WORD BY WORD

Second Edition

ENGLISH/ HAITIAN KREYOL

DIKSYONNÈ ANGLE AK PÒTRE

Steven J. Molinsky • Bill Bliss

Edwidge Crevecoeur-Bryant, Translator

Illustrated by
Richard E. Hill

PEARSON
Longman

Word by Word Picture Dictionary,
English/Haitian Kreyol second edition

Copyright © 2007 by Prentice Hall Regents
Pearson Education, Inc.
All rights reserved.
No part of this publication may be reproduced, stored in
a retrieval system, or transmitted in any form or by any
means, electronic, mechanical, photocopying, recording, or
otherwise, without the prior permission of the publisher.

Pearson Education, 10 Bank Street, White Plains, NY 10606

Editorial director: Pam Fishman
Vice president, director of design and
production: Rhea Banker
Director of electronic production: Aliza Greenblatt
Director of manufacturing: Patrice Fraccio
Senior manufacturing manager: Edith Pullman
Marketing manager: Oliva Fernandez
Editorial assistant: Katherine Keyes
Senior digital layout specialist: Wendy Wolf

Text design: Wendy Wolf
Cover design: Tracey Munz Cataldo
Realia creation: Warren Fischbach, Paula Williams
Illustrations: Richard E. Hill
Contributing artists: Steven Young, Charles Cawley,
Willard Gage, Marlon Violette
Reviewers: Jean-Claude Borgella, Miami Dade Public
Schools, Miami, Florida; Roland Crevecoeur, Florida School
for the Deaf and the Blind at St. Augustine
Project management by TransPac Education Services,
Victoria, BC, Canada with assistance from Yu Jian Yo,
Studio G & Robert Zacharias

ISBN 0-13-191627-0
Longman on the Web
Longman.com offers online resources for teachers and
students. Access our Companion Websites, our online
catalog, and our local offices around the world.

Visit us at longman.com.

Printed in the United States of America
6 2024

CONTENTS

SA KI NAN LIV SA A

Unit / Theme	Communication Skills	Writing & Discussion
1 Personal Information and Family	• Asking for & giving personal information • Identifying information on a form • Spelling name aloud • Identifying family members • Introducing others	• Telling about yourself • Telling about family members • Drawing a family tree
2 Common Everyday Activities and Language	• Identifying classroom objects & locations • Identifying classroom actions • Giving & following simple classroom commands • Identifying everyday & leisure activities • Inquiring by phone about a person's activities • Asking about a person's plan for future activities • Social communication: Greeting people, Leave taking, Introducing yourself & others, Getting someone's attention, Expressing gratitude, Saying you don't understand, Calling someone on the telephone • Describing the weather • Interpreting temperatures on a thermometer (Fahrenheit & Centigrade) • Describing the weather forecast for tomorrow	• Describing a classroom • Making a list of daily activities • Describing daily routine • Making a list of planned activities • Describing favorite leisure activities • Describing the weather
3 Numbers/ Time/ Money/ Calendar	• Using cardinal & ordinal numbers • Giving information about age, number of family members, residence • Telling time • Indicating time of events • Asking for information about arrival & departure times • Identifying coins & currency – names & values • Making & asking for change • Identifying days of the week • Identifying months of the year • Asking about the year, month, day, date • Asking about the date of a birthday, anniversary, appointment • Giving date of birth	• Describing numbers of students in a class • Identifying a country's population • Describing daily schedule with times • Telling about time management • Telling about the use of time in different cultures or countries • Describing the cost of purchases • Describing coins & currency of other countries • Describing weekday & weekend activities • Telling about favorite day of the week & month of the year
4 Home	• Identifying types of housing & communities • Requesting a taxi • Calling 911 for an ambulance • Identifying rooms of a home • Identifying furniture • Complimenting • Asking for information in a store • Locating items in a store • Asking about items on sale • Asking the location of items at home • Telling about past weekend activities • Identifying locations in an apartment building • Identifying ways to look for housing: classified ads, listings, vacancy signs • Renting an apartment • Describing household problems • Securing home repair services • Making a suggestion • Identifying household cleaning items, home supplies, & tools • Asking to borrow an item • Describing current home activities & plans for future activities	• Describing types of housing where people live • Describing rooms & furniture in a residence • Telling about baby products & early child-rearing practices in different countries • Telling about personal experiences with repairing things • Describing an apartment building • Describing household cleaning chores
5 Community	• Identifying places in the community • Exchanging greetings • Asking & giving the location of places in the community • Identifying government buildings, services, & other places in a city/town center • Identifying modes of transportation in a city/town center	• Describing places in a neighborhood • Making a list of places, people, & actions observed at an intersection

Unit / Theme	Communication Skills	Writing & Discussion
6 **Describing**	• Describing people by age • Describing people by physical characteristics • Describing a suspect or missing person to a police officer • Describing people & things using adjectives • Describing physical states & emotions • Expressing concern about another person's physical state or emotion	• Describing physical characteristics of yourself & family members • Describing physical characteristics of a favorite actor or actress or other famous person • Describing things at home & in the community • Telling about personal experiences with different emotions
7 **Food**	• Identifying food items (fruits, vegetables, meat, poultry, seafood, dairy products, juices, beverages, deli, frozen foods, snack foods, groceries) • Identifying non-food items purchased in a supermarket (e.g., household supplies, baby products, pet food) • Determining food needs to make a shopping list • Asking the location of items in a supermarket • Identifying supermarket sections • Requesting items at a service counter in a supermarket • Identifying supermarket checkout area personnel & items • Identifying food containers & quantities • Identifying units of measure • Asking for & giving recipe instructions • Complimenting someone on a recipe • Offering to help with food preparation • Identifying food preparation actions • Identifying kitchen utensils & cookware • Asking to borrow an item • Comprehending product advertising • Ordering fast food items, coffee shop items, & sandwiches • Indicating a shortage of supplies to a co-worker or supervisor • Taking customers' orders at a food service counter • Identifying restaurant objects, personnel, & actions • Making & following requests at work • Identifying & correctly positioning silverware & plates in a table setting • Inquiring in person about restaurant job openings • Ordering from a restaurant menu • Taking customers' orders as a waiter or waitress in a restaurant	• Describing favorite & least favorite foods • Describing foods in different countries • Making a shopping list • Describing places to shop for food • Telling about differences between supermarkets & food stores in different countries • Making a list of items in kitchen cabinets & the refrigerator • Describing recycling practices • Describing a favorite recipe using units of measure • Telling about use of kitchen utensils & cookware • Telling about experience with different types of restaurants • Describing restaurants and menus in different countries • Describing favorite foods ordered in restaurants
8 **Colors and Clothing**	• Identifying colors • Complimenting someone on clothing • Identifying clothing items, including outerwear, sleepwear, underwear, exercise clothing, footwear, jewelry, & accessories • Talking about appropriate clothing for different weather conditions • Expressing clothing needs to a store salesperson • Locating clothing items • Inquiring about ownership of found clothing items • Indicating loss of a clothing item • Asking about sale prices in a clothing store • Reporting theft of a clothing item to the police • Stating preferences during clothing shopping • Expressing problems with clothing & the need for alterations • Identifying laundry objects & activities • Locating laundry products in a store	• Describing the flags of different countries • Telling about emotions associated with different colors • Telling about clothing & colors you like to wear • Describing clothing worn at different occasions (e.g., going to schools, parties, weddings) • Telling about clothing worn in different weather conditions • Telling about clothing worn during exercise activities • Telling about footwear worn during different activities • Describing the color, material, size, & pattern of favorite clothing items • Comparing clothing fashions now & a long time ago • Telling about who does laundry at home

Unit / Theme	Communication Skills	Writing & Discussion
9 Shopping	• Identifying departments & services in a department store • Asking the location of items in a department store • Asking to buy, return, exchange, try on, & pay for department store items • Asking about regular & sales prices, discounts, & sales tax • Interpreting a sales receipt • Offering assistance to customers as a salesperson • Expressing needs to a salesperson in a store • Identifying electronics products, including video & audio equipment, telephones, cameras, & computers • Identifying components of a computer & common computer software • Complimenting someone about an item & inquiring where it was purchased • Asking a salesperson for advice about different brands of a product • Identifying common toys & other items in a toy store • Asking for advice about an appropriate gift for a child	• Describing a department store • Telling about stores that have sales • Telling about an item purchased on sale • Comparing different types & brands of video & audio equipment • Describing telephones & cameras • Describing personal use of a computer • Sharing opinions about how computers have changed the world • Telling about popular toys in different countries • Telling about favorite childhood toys
10 Community Services	• Requesting bank services & transactions (e.g., deposit, withdrawal, cashing a check, obtaining traveler's checks, opening an account, applying for a loan, exchanging currency) • Identifying bank personnel • Identifying bank forms • Asking about acceptable forms of payment (cash, check, credit card, money order, traveler's check) • Identifying household bills (rent, utilities, etc.) • Identifying family finance documents & actions • Following instructions to use an ATM machine • Requesting post office services & transactions • Identifying types of mail & mail services • Identifying different ways to buy stamps • Requesting non-mail services available at the post office (money order, selective service registration, passport application) • Identifying & locating library sections, services, & personnel • Asking how to find a book in the library • Identifying community institutions, services, and personnel (police, fire, city government, public works, recreation, sanitation, religious institutions) • Identifying types of emergency vehicles • Reporting a crime • Identifying community mishaps (gas leak, water main break, etc.) • Expressing concern about community problems	• Describing use of bank services • Telling about household bills & amounts paid • Telling about the person responsible for household finances • Describing use of ATM machines • Describing use of postal services • Comparing postal systems in different countries • Telling about experience using a library • Telling about the location of community institutions • Describing experiences using community institutions • Telling about crime in the community • Describing experience with a crime or emergency
11 Health	• Identifying parts of the body & key internal organs • Describing ailments, symptoms, & injuries • Asking about the health of another person • Identifying items in a first-aid kit • Describing medical emergencies • Identifying emergency medical procedures (CPR, rescue breathing, Heimlich maneuver) • Calling 911 to report a medical emergency • Identifying major illnesses • Talking with a friend or co-worker about illness in one's family • Following instructions during a medical examination • Identifying medical personnel, equipment, & supplies in medical & dental offices • Understanding medical & dental personnel's description of procedures during treatment • Understanding a doctor's medical advice and instructions • Identifying over-the-counter medications • Understanding dosage instructions on medicine labels • Identifying medical specialists • Indicating the date & time of a medical appointment • Identifying hospital departments & personnel • Identifying equipment in a hospital room • Identifying actions & items related to personal hygiene • Locating personal care products in a store • Identifying actions & items related to baby care	• Describing self • Telling about a personal experience with an illness or injury • Describing remedies or treatments for common problems (cold, stomachache, insect bite, hiccups) • Describing experience with a medical emergency • Describing a medical examination • Describing experience with a medical or dental procedure • Telling about medical advice received • Telling about over-the-counter medications used • Comparing use of medications in different countries • Describing experience with a medical specialist • Describing a hospital stay • Making a list of personal care items needed for a trip • Comparing baby products in different countries

Unit / Theme	Communication Skills	Writing & Discussion

12 **School, Subjects, and Activities**	• Identifying types of educational institutions
	• Giving information about previous education during a job interview
	• Identifying school locations & personnel
	• Identifying school subjects
	• Identifying extracurricular activities
	• Sharing after-school plans
	• MATH:
	  • Asking & answering basic questions during a math class
	  • Using fractions to indicate sale prices
	  • Using percents to indicate test scores & probability in weather forecasts
	  • Identifying high school math subjects
	  • Using measurement terms to indicate height, width, depth, length, distance
	  • Interpreting metric measurements
	  • Identifying types of lines, geometric shapes, & solid figures
	• ENGLISH LANGUAGE ARTS:
	  • Identifying types of sentences
	  • Identifying parts of speech
	  • Identifying punctuation marks
	  • Providing feedback during peer-editing
	  • Identifying steps of the writing process
	  • Identifying types of literature
	  • Identifying forms of writing
	• GEOGRAPHY:
	  • Identifying geographical features & bodies of water
	  • Identifying natural environments (desert, jungle, rainforest, etc.)
	• SCIENCE:
	  • Identifying science classroom/laboratory equipment
	  • Asking about equipment needed to do a science procedure
	  • Identifying steps of the scientific method
	  • Identifying key terms to describe the universe, solar system, & space exploration
		• Telling about different types of schools in the community
		• Telling about schools attended, where, when, & subjects studied
		• Describing a school
		• Comparing schools in different countries
		• Telling about favorite school subject
		• Telling about extracurricular activities
		• Comparing extracurricular activities in different countries
		• Describing math education
		• Telling about something bought on sale
		• Researching & sharing information about population statistics using percents
		• Describing favorite books & authors
		• Describing newspapers & magazines read
		• Telling about use of different types of written communication
		• Describing the geography of your country
		• Describing geographical features experienced
		• Describing experience with scientific equipment
		• Describing science education
		• Brainstorming a science experiment & describing each step of the scientific method
		• Drawing & naming a constellation
		• Expressing an opinion about the importance of space exploration

13 **Work**	• Identifying occupations • Stating work experience (including length of time in an occupation) during a job interview • Talking about occupation during social conversation • Expressing job aspirations • Identifying job skills & work activities • Indicating job skills during an interview (including length of time) • Identifying types of job advertisements (help wanted signs, job notices, classified ads) • Interpreting abbreviations in job advertisements • Identifying each step in a job-search process • Identifying workplace locations, furniture, equipment, & personnel • Identifying common office tasks • Asking the location of a co-worker • Engaging in small-talk with co-workers • Identifying common office supplies • Making requests at work • Repeating to confirm understanding of a request or instruction • Identifying factory locations, equipment, & personnel • Asking the location of workplace departments & personnel to orient oneself as a new employee • Asking about the location & activities of a co-worker • Identifying construction site machinery, equipment, and building materials • Asking a co-worker for a workplace item • Warning a co-worker of a safety hazard • Asking whether there is a sufficient supply of workplace materials • Identifying job safety equipment • Interpreting warning signs at work • Reminding someone to use safety equipment • Asking the location of emergency equipment at work	• Career exploration: sharing ideas about occupations that are interesting, difficult • Describing occupation & occupations of family members • Describing job skills • Describing a familiar job (skill requirements, qualifications, hours, salary) • Telling about how people found their jobs • Telling about experience with a job search or job interview • Describing a familiar workplace • Telling about office & school supplies used • Describing a nearby factory & working conditions there • Comparing products produced by factories in different countries • Describing building materials used in ones dwelling • Describing a nearby construction site • Telling about experience with safety equipment • Describing the use of safety equipment in the community

Unit / Theme	Communication Skills	Writing & Discussion
14 **Transportation and Travel**	• Identifying modes of local & inter-city public transportation • Expressing intended mode of travel • Asking about a location to obtain transportation (bus stop, bus station, train station, subway station) • Locating ticket counters, information booths, fare card machines, & information signage in transportation stations • Identifying types of vehicles • Indicating to a car salesperson need for a type of vehicle • Describing a car accident • Identifying parts of a car & maintenance items • Indicating a problem with a car • Requesting service or assistance at a service station • Identifying types of highway lanes & markings, road structures (tunnels, bridges, etc.), traffic signage, & local intersection road markings • Reporting the location of an accident • Giving & following driving directions (using prepositions of motion) • Interpreting traffic signs • Warning a driver about an upcoming sign • Interpreting compass directions • Asking for driving directions • Following instructions during a driver's test • Repeating to confirm instructions • Identifying airport locations & personnel (check-in, security, gate, baggage claim, Customs & Immigration) • Asking for location of places & personnel at an airport • Indicating loss of travel documents or other items • Identifying airplane sections, seating areas, emergency equipment, & flight personnel • Identifying steps in the process of airplane travel (actions in the security area, at the gate, boarding, & being seated) • Following instructions of airport security personnel, gate attendants, & flight crew • Identifying sections of a hotel & personnel • Asking for location of places & personnel in a hotel	• Describing mode of travel to different places in the community • Describing local public transportation • Comparing transportation in different countries • Telling about common types of vehicles in different countries • Expressing opinion about favorite type of vehicle & manufacturer • Expressing opinion about most important features to look for when making a car purchase • Describing experience with car repairs • Describing a local highway • Describing a local intersection • Telling about dangerous traffic areas where many accidents occur • Describing your route from home to school • Describing how to get to different places from home and school • Describing local traffic signs • Comparing traffic signs in different countries • Describing a familiar airport • Telling about an experience with Customs & Immigration • Describing an air travel experience • Using imagination: being an airport security officer giving passengers instructions; being a flight attendant giving passengers instructions before take-off • Describing a familiar hotel • Expressing opinion about hotel jobs that are most interesting, most difficult
15 **Recreation and Entertainment**	• Identifying common hobbies, crafts, & games & related materials/equipment • Describing favorite leisure activities • Purchasing craft supplies, equipment, & other products in a store • Asking for & offering a suggestion for a leisure activity • Identifying places to go for outdoor recreation, entertainment, culture, etc. • Describing past weekend activities • Describing activities planned for a future day off or weekend • Identifying features & equipment in a park & playground • Asking the location of a park feature or equipment • Warning a child to be careful on playground equipment • Identifying features of a beach, common beach items, & personnel • Identifying indoor & outdoor recreation activities & sports, & related equipment & supplies • Asking if someone remembered an item when preparing for an activity • Identifying team sports & terms for players, playing fields, & equipment • Commenting on a player's performance during a game • Indicating that you can't find an item • Asking the location of sports equipment in a store • Reminding someone of items needed for a sports activity • Identifying types of winter/water sports, recreation, & equipment • Engaging in small talk about favorite sports & recreation activities • Using the telephone to inquire whether a store sells a product • Making & responding to an invitation • Following a teacher or coach's instructions during sports practice, P.E. class, & an exercise class • Identifying types of entertainment & cultural events, & the performers • Commenting on a performance • Identifying genres of music, plays, movies, & TV programs • Expressing likes about types of entertainment • Identifying musical instruments • Complimenting someone on musical ability	• Describing a favorite hobby, craft, or game • Comparing popular games in different countries, and how to play them • Describing favorite places to go & activities there • Describing a local park & playground • Describing a favorite beach & items used there • Describing an outdoor recreation experience • Describing favorite individual sports & recreation activities • Describing favorite team sports & famous players • Comparing popular sports in different countries • Describing experience with winter or water sports & recreation • Expressing opinions about Winter Olympics sports (most exciting, most dangerous) • Describing exercise habits & routines • Using imagination: being an exercise instructor leading a class • Telling about favorite types of entertainment • Comparing types of entertainment popular in different countries • Telling about favorite performers • Telling about favorite types of music, movies, & TV programs • Describing experience with a musical instrument • Comparing typical musical instruments in different countries

Unit / Theme	Communication Skills	Writing & Discussion
16 Nature	• Identifying places & people on a farm • Identifying farm animals & crops • Identifying animals & pets • Identifying birds & insects • Identifying fish, sea animals, amphibians, & reptiles • Asking about the presence of wildlife in an area • Identifying trees, plants, & flowers • Identifying key parts of a tree and flower • Asking for information about trees & flowers • Warning someone about poisonous vegetation in an area • Identifying sources of energy • Describing the kind of energy used to heat homes & for cooking • Expressing an opinion about good future sources of energy • Identifying behaviors that promote conservation (recycling, conserving energy, conserving water, carpooling) • Expressing concern about environmental problems • Identifying different kinds of natural disasters	• Comparing farms in different countries • Telling about local animals, animals in a zoo, & common local birds & insects • Comparing common pets in different countries • Using imagination: what animal you would like to be, & why • Telling a popular folk tale or children's story about animals, birds, or insects • Describing fish, sea animals, & reptiles in different countries • Identifying endangered species • Expressing opinions about wildlife – most interesting, beautiful, dangerous • Describing local trees & flowers, & favorites • Comparing different cultures' use of flowers at weddings, funerals, holidays, & hospitals • Expressing an opinion about an environmental problem • Telling about how people prepare for natural disasters
17 U.S. Civics	• Producing correct form of identification when requested (driver's license, social security card, student I.D. card, employee I.D. badge, permanent resident card, passport, visa, work permit, birth certificate, proof of residence) • Identifying the three branches of U.S. government (legislative, executive, judicial) & their functions • Identifying senators, representatives, the president, vice-president, cabinet, Supreme Court justices, & the chief justice, & the branches of government in which they work • Identifying the key buildings in each branch of government (Capitol Building, White House, Supreme Court Building) • Identifying the Constitution as "the supreme law of the land" • Identifying the Bill of Rights • Naming freedoms guaranteed by the 1st Amendment • Identifying key amendments to the Constitution • Identifying key events in United States history • Answering history questions about events and the dates they occurred • Identifying key holidays & dates they occur • Identifying legal system & court procedures (arrest, booking, obtaining legal representation, appearing in court, standing trial, acquittal, conviction, sentencing, prison, release) • Identifying people in the criminal justice system • Engaging in small talk about a TV crime show's characters & plot • Identifying rights & responsibilities of U.S. citizens • Identifying steps in applying for citizenship	• Telling about forms of identification & when needed • Describing how people in a community "exercise their 1st Amendment rights" • Brainstorming ideas for a new amendment to the Constitution • Expressing an opinion about the most important event in United States history • Telling about important events in the history of different countries • Describing U.S. holidays you celebrate • Describing holidays celebrated in different countries • Describing the legal system in different countries • Telling about an episode of a TV crime show • Expressing an opinion about the most important rights & responsibilities of people in their communities • Expressing an opinion about the rights of citizens vs. non-citizens

Welcome to the second edition of the WORD BY WORD Picture Dictionary! This text presents more than 4,000 vocabulary words through vibrant illustrations and simple accessible lesson pages that are designed for clarity and ease-of-use with learners at all levels. Our goal is to prepare students for success using English in everyday life, in the community, in school, and at work.

WORD BY WORD organizes the vocabulary into 17 thematic units, providing a careful research-based sequence of lessons that integrates students' development of grammar and vocabulary skills through topics that begin with the immediate world of the student and progress to the world at large. Early lessons on the family, the home, and daily activities lead to lessons on the community, school, workplace, shopping, recreation, and other topics. The text offers extensive coverage of important lifeskill competencies and the vocabulary of school subjects and extracurricular activities, and it is designed to meet the objectives of current national, state, and local standards-based curricula you can find in the Scope & Sequence on the previous pages.

Since each lesson in *Word by Word* is self-contained, it can be used either sequentially or in any desired order. For users' convenience, the lessons are listed in two ways: sequentially in the Table of Contents, and alphabetically in the Thematic Index. These resources, combined with the Glossary in the appendix, allow students and teachers to quickly and easily locate all words and topics in the Picture Dictionary.

The *Word by Word* Picture Dictionary is the centerpiece of the complete *Word by Word* Vocabulary Development Program, which offers a wide selection of print and media support materials for instruction at all levels.

A unique choice of workbooks at Beginning and Intermediate levels offers flexible options to meet students' needs. Vocabulary Workbooks feature motivating vocabulary, grammar, and listening practice, and standards-based Lifeskills Workbooks provide competency-based activities and reading tied to national, state, and local curriculum frameworks. A Literacy Workbook is also available.

The Teacher's Guide and Lesson Planner with CD-ROM includes lesson-planning suggestions, community tasks, Internet weblinks, and reproducible masters to save teachers hours of lesson preparation time. An Activity Handbook with step-by-step teaching strategies for key vocabulary development activities is included in the Teacher's Guide.

The Audio Program includes all words and conversations for interactive practice and —as bonus material—an expanded selection of WordSongs for entertaining musical practice with the vocabulary.

Additional ancillary materials include Color Transparencies, Vocabulary Game Cards, and a Testing Program. Bilingual Editions are also available.

Teaching Strategies

Word by Word presents vocabulary words in context. Model conversations depict situations in which people use the words in meaningful communication. These models become the basis for students to engage in dynamic, interactive practice. In addition, writing and discussion questions in each lesson encourage students to relate the vocabulary and themes to their own lives as they share experiences, thoughts, opinions, and information about themselves, their cultures, and their countries. In this way, students get to know each other "word by word."

In using *Word by Word*, we encourage you to develop approaches and strategies that are compatible with your own teaching style and the needs and abilities of your students. You may find it helpful to incorporate some of the following techniques for presenting and practicing the vocabulary in each lesson.

1. **Preview the Vocabulary:** Activate students' prior knowledge of the vocabulary by brainstorming with students the words in the lesson they already know and writing them on the board, or by having students look at the transparency or the illustration in *Word by Word* and identify the words they are familiar with.

2. **Present the Vocabulary:** Using the transparency or the illustration in the Picture Dictionary, point to the picture of each word, say the word, and have the class repeat it chorally and individually. (You can also play the word list on the Audio Program.) Check students' understanding and pronunciation of the vocabulary.

3. **Vocabulary Practice:** Have students practice the vocabulary as a class, in pairs, or in small groups. Say or write a word, and have students point to the item or tell the number. Or, point to an item or give the number, and have students say the word.

4. **Model Conversation Practice:** Some lessons have model conversations that use the first word in the vocabulary list. Other models are in the form of skeletal dialogs, in which vocabulary words can be inserted. (In many skeletal dialogs, bracketed numbers indicate which words can be used for practicing the conversation. If no bracketed numbers appear, all the words in the lesson can be used.)

The following steps are recommended for Model Conversation Practice:

a. **Preview:** Have students look at the model illustration and discuss who they think the speakers are and where the conversation takes place.

b. The teacher presents the model or plays the audio one or more times and checks students' understanding of the situation and the vocabulary.

c. Students repeat each line of the conversation chorally and individually.

d. Students practice the model in pairs.

e. A pair of students presents a conversation based on the model, but using a different word from the vocabulary list.

f. In pairs, students practice several conversations based on the model, using different words on the page.

g. Pairs present their conversations to the class.

5. **Additional Conversation Practice:** Many lessons provide two additional skeletal dialogs for further conversation practice with the vocabulary. (These can be found in the yellow-shaded area at the bottom of the page.) Have students practice and present these conversations using any words they wish. Before they practice the additional conversations, you may want to have students listen to the sample additional conversations on the Audio Program.

6. **Spelling Practice:** Have students practice spelling the words as a class, in pairs, or in small groups. Say a word, and have students spell it aloud or write it. Or, using the transparency, point to an item and have students write the word.

7. **Themes for Discussion, Composition, Journals, and Portfolios:** Each lesson of *Word by Word* provides one or more questions for discussion and composition. (These can be found in a blue-shaded area at the bottom of the page.) Have students respond to the questions as a class, in pairs, or in small groups. Or, have students write their responses at home, share their written work with other students, and discuss as a class, in pairs, or in small groups.

Students may enjoy keeping a journal of their written work. If time permits, you may want to write a response in each student's journal, sharing your own opinions and experiences as well as reacting to what the student has written. If you are keeping portfolios of students' work, these compositions serve as excellent examples of students' progress in learning English.

8. **Communication Activities:** The *Word by Word* Teacher's Guide and Lesson Planner with CD-ROM provides a wealth of games, tasks, brainstorming, discussion, movement, drawing, miming, role-playing, and other activities designed to take advantage of students' different learning styles and particular abilities and strengths. For each lesson, choose one or more of these activities to reinforce students' vocabulary learning in a way that is stimulating, creative, and enjoyable.

WORD BY WORD aims to offer students a communicative, meaningful, and lively way of practicing English vocabulary. In conveying to you the substance of our program, we hope that we have also conveyed the spirit: that learning vocabulary can be genuinely interactive . . . relevant to our students' lives . . . responsive to students' differing strengths and learning styles . . . and fun!

Steven J. Molinsky
Bill Bliss

ENFÒMASYON PÈSONNÈL

Registration Form

Name: Gloria (First) P. (Middle Initial) Sánchez (Last)

Address: 95 (Number) Garden Street (Street) 3G (Apartment Number)
Los Angeles (City) CA (State) 90036 (Zip Code)

Telephone: 323-524-3278   Cell Phone: 323-695-1864

E-Mail Address: gloria97@ail.com   SSN: 227-93-6185   Sex M__ F X

Date of Birth: 5/12/88   Place of Birth: Centerville, Texas

Kreyòl	#	English
non	1	name
prenmyè non	2	first name
dezyèm non	3	middle initial
dènye non/ siyati/tinon gate	4	last name/family name/ surname
adrès/kote ou rete	5	address
nimewo apatman/ nimewo kay	6	street number
ri/lari	7	street
nimewo apatman	8	apartment number
vil/lavil	9	city
eta	10	state
kòd postal	11	zip code
areyakòd	12	area code
nimewo telefòn	13	telephone number/ phone number
nimewo selilè	14	cell phone number
adrès emèl	15	e-mail address
nimewo sosyal	16	social security number
sèks	17	sex
dat ou fèt	18	date of birth
kote ou fèt	19	place of birth

A. What's your **name**?
B. Gloria P. Sánchez.

A. What's your _____?
B. ....
A. Did you say ....?
B. Yes. That's right.

A. What's your last name?
B. ....
A. How do you spell that?
B. ....

Tell about yourself:
My name is ....
My address is ....
My telephone number is ....

Now interview a friend.

mari	**1**	husband	timoun yo	**children**	gran paran yo	**grandparents**
madanm	**2**	wife	pitit fi	**5** daughter	grann	**10** grandmother
			pitit gason	**6** son	granpapa	**11** grandfather
paran yo		**parents**	bebe	**7** baby		
papa	**3**	father			pitit pitit yo	**grandchildren**
manman	**4**	mother	frè ak sè	**siblings**	pitit pitit fi	**12** granddaughter
			sè	**8** sister	pitit pitit gason	**13** grandson
			frè	**9** brother		

A. Who is he?
B. He's my **husband**.
A. What's his name?
B. His name is *Jack*.

A. Who is she?
B. She's my **wife**.
A. What's her name?
B. Her name is *Nancy*.

A. I'd like to introduce my _____.
B. Nice to meet you.
C. Nice to meet you, too.

A. What's your _____'s name?
B. His/Her name is ....

Who are the people in your family?
What are their names?

Tell about photos of family members.

MOUN KI NAN LAFANMI II

Helen   Walter

Jack   Nancy   Frank   Linda

Jennifer   Timmy   Alan

tonton/monnonk	**1**	uncle		bèlmè	**6**	mother-in-law
tant/matant	**2**	aunt		bòpè	**7**	father-in-law
nyès	**3**	niece		bofis	**8**	son-in-law
neve	**4**	nephew		bèlfi	**9**	daughter-in-law
kouzen/kouzin	**5**	cousin		bòfrè	**10**	brother-in-law
				bèlsè	**11**	sister-in-law

① Jack is Alan's ____.

② Nancy is Alan's ____.

③ Jennifer is Frank and Linda's ____.

④ Timmy is Frank and Linda's ____.

⑤ Alan is Jennifer and Timmy's ____.

⑥ Helen is Jack's ____.

⑦ Walter is Jack's ____.

⑧ Jack is Helen and Walter's ____.

⑨ Linda is Helen and Walter's ____.

⑩ Frank is Jack's ____.

⑪ Linda is Jack's ____.

A. Who is he/she?

B. He's/She's my _____.

A. What's his/her name?

B. His/Her name is _____.

A. Let me introduce my _____.

B. I'm glad to meet you.

C. Nice meeting you, too.

Tell about your relatives:
  What are their names?
  Where do they live?

Draw your family tree and tell about it.

THE CLASSROOM
SALDEKLAS LA

pwofesè	**1**	teacher	pwojektè fim transparan	**8**	overhead projector	
èd pwofesè	**2**	teacher's aide				
elèv	**3**	student	ekran	**9**	screen	
biwo	**4**	desk	tablo	**10**	chalkboard/board	
chèz	**5**	seat/chair	pandil	**11**	clock	
tab	**6**	table	kat jewografi	**12**	map	
konpitè	**7**	computer	tablo pou afich	**13**	bulletin board	
			wopalè	**14**	P.A. system/loudspeaker	

tablo blan	**15**	whiteboard/board
glòb lemonn/glòb tèrès	**16**	globe
etajè liv	**17**	bookcase/bookshelf
biwo pwofesè	**18**	teacher's desk
kòbèy papye	**19**	wastebasket

plim	**20**	pen	klasè	**27**	binder/notebook
kreyon	**21**	pencil	papye delin	**28**	notebook paper
gòm	**22**	eraser	papye kawo	**29**	graph paper
tay kreyon/egize	**23**	pencil sharpener	règ	**30**	ruler
liv lekòl	**24**	book/textbook	kalkilatè	**31**	calculator
liv egzèsis	**25**	workbook	lakre	**32**	chalk
kaye nòt	**26**	spiral notebook	chifon	**33**	eraser

makè	**34**	marker
klou pinèz	**35**	thumbtack
klavye	**36**	keyboard
monitè	**37**	monitor
sourit	**38**	mouse
enprimant	**39**	printer

A. Where's the **teacher**?
B. The **teacher** is *next to* the **board**.

A. Where's the **globe**?
B. The **globe** is *on* the **bookcase**.

A. Is there a/an _____ in your classroom?*
B. Yes. There's a/an _____
   next to/on the _____.

A. Is there a/an _____ in your classroom?*
B. No, there isn't.

Describe your classroom.
(There's a/an ....)

* With 28, 29, 32 use: Is there _____ in your classroom?

AKTIVITE NAN KLAS

Di non ou.	**1** Say your name.	Leve men ou.	**16** Raise your hand.
Repete non ou.	**2** Repeat your name.	Mande yon kesyon.	**17** Ask a question.
Eple non ou.	**3** Spell your name.	Koute kesyon an.	**18** Listen to the question.
Ekri non ou detache.	**4** Print your name.	Reponn kesyon an.	**19** Answer the question.
Siyen non ou	**5** Sign your name.	Koute repons lan.	**20** Listen to the answer.
Kanpe.	**6** Stand up.	Fè devwa ou.	**21** Do your homework.
Ale sou tablo a	**7** Go to the board.	Pote devwa ou	**22** Bring in your homework.
Ekri sou tablo a.	**8** Write on the board.	Repase repons yo	**23** Go over the answers.
Efase tablo a.	**9** Erase the board.	Korije fòt ou yo.	**24** Correct your mistakes.
Chita/Pran plas ou.	**10** Sit down./Take your seat.	Renmèt devwa ou.	**25** Hand in your homework.
Louvri liv ou.	**11** Open your book.	Pataje liv la.	**26** Share a book.
Li paj dis.	**12** Read page ten.	Diskite kesyon an.	**27** Discuss the question.
Etidye paj dis.	**13** Study page ten.	Youn ede lòt.	**28** Help each other.
Fèmen liv ou.	**14** Close your book.	Travay ansanm.	**29** Work together.
Ranmase liv ou.	**15** Put away your book.	Pataje ak klas la.	**30** Share with the class.

Chèche nan diksyonè a.	31	Look in the dictionary.		Pase fèy egzamen yo.	47	Pass out the tests.
Chèche yon mo.	32	Look up a word.		Reponn kesyon yo.	48	Answer the questions.
Pwonnonse mo a.	33	Pronounce the word.		Tcheke repons yo.	49	Check your answers.
Li definisyon an.	34	Read the definition.		Ranmase egzamen yo.	50	Collect the tests.
Kopye mo a.	35	Copy the word.		Chwazi repons ki pi bon an.	51	Choose the correct answer.
Travay poukont ou.	36	Work alone./ Do your own work.		Mete yon wonn nan repons ki pi bon an.	52	Circle the correct answer.
Travay ak yonlòt/asosye.	37	Work with a partner.		Ekri nan espas vid la.	53	Fill in the blank.
Separe an ti gwoup.	38	Break up into small groups.		Make repons lan sou papye.	54	Mark the answer sheet./ Bubble the answer.
Travay an gwoup.	39	Work in a group.		Konekte mo yo.	55	Match the words.
Travay ansanm.	40	Work as a class.		Pase yon trè anba mo a.	56	Underline the word.
Desann rido yo.	41	Lower the shades.		Pase yon kwa sou mo a.	57	Cross out the word.
Etèn limyè yo.	42	Turn off the lights.		Demelanje mo yo.	58	Unscramble the word.
Gade ekran.	43	Look at the screen.		Mete mo yo an nòd.	59	Put the words in order.
Pran nòt.	44	Take notes.		Ekri nan yon lòt papye.	60	Write on a separate sheet of paper.
Limen limyè yo.	45	Turn on the lights.				
Retire yon fèy papye.	46	Take out a piece of paper.				

You're the teacher! Give instructions to your students!

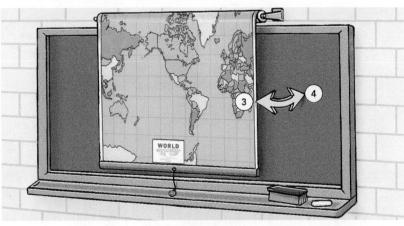

anlè	**1** above	sou kote	**5** next to	adwat	**9** to the right of
anba	**2** below	sou	**6** on	anndan	**10** in
devan	**3** in front of	anba	**7** under	nan mitan	**11** between
dèyè	**4** behind	agoch	**8** to the left of		

[1–10]
A. Where's the *clock*?
B. The *clock* is **above** the *bulletin board*.

[11]
A. Where's the *dictionary*?
B. The *dictionary* is **between** the *globe* and the *pencil sharpener*.

Tell about the classroom on page 4. Use the prepositions in this lesson.

Tell about your classroom.

AKTIVITE TOULEJOU I

leve	**1** get up	dezabiye	**11** get undressed
pran yon douch	**2** take a shower	benyen	**12** take a bath
bwose dan *mwen**	**3** brush *my** teeth	ale kouche	**13** go to bed
fè labab	**4** shave	dòmi	**14** sleep
abiye	**5** get dressed	fè manje maten	**15** make breakfast
lave figi *mwen**	**6** wash *my** face	fè manje midi/lench	**16** make lunch
makiye	**7** put on makeup	fè manje aswè	**17** cook/make dinner
bwose tèt *mwen**	**8** brush *my** hair	manje manje maten	**18** eat/have breakfast
penyen tèt *mwen**	**9** comb *my** hair	manje midi/lench	**19** eat/have lunch
fè kabann nan	**10** make the bed	manje aswè	**20** eat/have dinner

* my, his, her, our, your, their

A. What do you do every day?
B. I **get up**, I **take a shower**, and I **brush my teeth**.

A. What does he do every day?
B. He _____s, he _____s, and he _____s.

A. What does she do every day?
B. She _____s, she _____s, and she_____s.

What do you do every day? Make a list.

Interview some friends and tell about their everyday activities.

EVERYDAY ACTIVITIES II

AKTIVITE TOULEJOU II

netwaye apatman an/	**1**	clean the apartment/	
netwaye kay la		clean the house	
lave vesèl la	**2**	wash the dishes	
fè lesiv	**3**	do the laundry	
pase fè	**4**	iron	
bay bebe a manje	**5**	feed the baby	
bay chat la manje	**6**	feed the cat	
pwonmennen chen an	**7**	walk the dog	
etidye	**8**	study	

al nan travay	**9**	go to work
al lekòl	**10**	go to school
kondui al travay	**11**	drive to work
pran bis pou ale lekòl	**12**	take the bus to school
travay	**13**	work
kite travay	**14**	leave work
al nan makèt	**15**	go to the store
vin lakay	**16**	come home/get home

A. Hello. What are you doing?
B. I'm **clean**ing the **apartment**.

A. Hello, ... This is ....
    What are you doing?
B. I'm _____ing. How about you?
A. I'm _____ing.

A. Are you going to _____ soon?
B. Yes. I'm going to _____ in a
    little while.

What are you going to do tomorrow?
Make a list of everything you are
going to do.

AKTIVITE LIB

gade televizyon	**1**	watch TV	jwe gita	**9**	play the guitar
koute radyo	**2**	listen to the radio	pratike pyano	**10**	practice the piano
tande mizik	**3**	listen to music	ekzèsis	**11**	exercise
li yon liv	**4**	read a book	naje	**12**	swim
li jounal	**5**	read the newspaper	plante flè	**13**	plant flowers
jwe	**6**	play	sèvi ak òdinatè	**14**	use the computer
jwe kat	**7**	play cards	ekri yon lèt	**15**	write a letter
jwe baskèt	**8**	play basketball	repoze	**16**	relax

A. Hi. What are you doing?
B. I'm **watch**ing **TV**.

A. Hi, ... Are you
_____ing?
B. No, I'm not. I'm _____ing.

A. What's your (husband/wife/son/
daughter/. . .) doing?
B. He's/She's _____ing.

What leisure activities do you like to do?

What do your family members and
friends like to do?

KONVÈSASYON TOULEJOU

Greeting People   Ap Salye Moun

Leave Taking   Ap Di Orevwa

Alo.	**1**	Hello. / Hi.
Bonjou.	**2**	Good morning.
Bòn apremidi.	**3**	Good afternoon.
Bonswa.	**4**	Good evening.
Kouman ou ye?	**5**	How are you? / How are you doing?
Byen. / Byen mèsi. / Pa mal.	**6**	Fine. / Fine, thanks. / Okay.

Sak nouvo kounye a? / Sak nouvo avè w kounye a?	**7**	What's new? / What's new with you?
Pa anpil. / Pa twò anpil.	**8**	Not much. / Not too much.
Orevwa.	**9**	Good-bye. / Bye.
Bònnwit.	**10**	Good night.
Na wè pi ta. / Na wè toutalè.	**11**	See you later. / See you soon.

Introducing Yourself and Others   Ap Prezante Ou Ba Lòt

Getting Someone's Attention
Ap Atire Atansyon Yon Moun

Expressing Gratitude
Ap Montre Rekonesans

Saying You Don't Understand
Ap Di Ou Pa Konprann.

Calling Someone on the Telephone
Ap Rele Yon Moun nan Telefòn

Alo. Mwen rele..../ Alo. M rele.........	**12**	Hello. My name is ..../ Hi. I'm ....
Mwen kontan fè konesans ou.	**13**	Nice to meet you.
Mwen kontan fè konesans ou tou.	**14**	Nice to meet you, too.
M ta renmen prezante ..../Se	**15**	I'd like to introduce ..../ This is ....
Eskize m.	**16**	Excuse me.
Èske mwen ka mande yon kesyon?	**17**	May I ask a question?

Mèsi.	**18**	Thank you./Thanks.
Padkwa.	**19**	You're welcome.
Mwen pa konprann./Eskize m. Mwen pa konprann.	**20**	I don't understand./ Sorry. I don't understand.
Èske ou ka repete l ankò?/ Èske ou ka dil ankò?	**21**	Can you please repeat that?/ Can you please say that again?
Alo. Se .... Èske m. ka pale ak ....?	**22**	Hello. This is .... May I please speak to ....?
Wi. Tann yon segonn.	**23**	Yes. Hold on a moment.
Eskize m. .... pa la kounye a.	**24**	I'm sorry. .... isn't here right now.

Practice conversations with other students. Use all the expressions on pages 12 and 13.

TAN

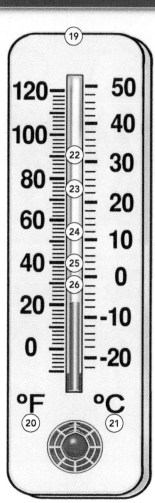

Tan		Weather
bèl solèy	1	sunny
nyaj kouvri	2	cloudy
fè klè	3	clear
tan sonm	4	hazy
gen bwouya	5	foggy
lafimen ak pousyè	6	smoggy
lap vante	7	windy
fè imid	8	humid/muggy
gen lapli	9	raining
lapli ap farinen	10	drizzling
gen nèj	11	snowing
gen grèl	12	hailing
lagrèl ap tonbe	13	sleeting

zeklè	14	lightning
loraj	15	thunderstorm
tanpèt nèj	16	snowstorm
tanpèt pousyè	17	dust storm
vag chalè	18	heat wave

Tanperatii		Temperature
tèmonmèt	19	thermometer
Farennayt	20	Fahrenheit
santigrad	21	Centigrade/Celsius
cho	22	hot
tyèd	23	warm
fre	24	cool
frèt	25	cold
glase	26	freezing

[1–13]
A. What's the weather like?
B. It's _____ .

[14–18]
A. What's the weather forecast?
B. There's going to be ___[14]___ /
a ___[15–18]___ .

[20–26]
A. How's the weather?
B. It's ___[22–26]___ .
A. What's the temperature?
B. It's . . . degrees ___[20–21]___ .

NIMEWO

Cardinal Numbers   Nimewo ki endike kantite

0 zero	11 eleven	21 twenty-one	101 one hundred (and) one
1 one	12 twelve	22 twenty-two	102 one hundred (and) two
2 two	13 thirteen	30 thirty	1,000 one thousand
3 three	14 fourteen	40 forty	10,000 ten thousand
4 four	15 fifteen	50 fifty	100,000 one hundred thousand
5 five	16 sixteen	60 sixty	1,000,000 one million
6 six	17 seventeen	70 seventy	1,000,000,000 one billion
7 seven	18 eighteen	80 eighty	
8 eight	19 nineteen	90 ninety	
9 nine	20 twenty	100 one hundred	
10 ten			

A. How old are you?
B. I'm _____ years old.

A. How many people are there in your family?
B. _____.

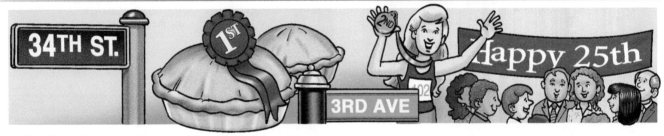

Ordinal Numbers   Nimewo ki endike lòd ranjman

1st first	11th eleventh	21st twenty-first	101st one hundred (and) first
2nd second	12th twelfth	22nd twenty-second	102nd one hundred (and) second
3rd third	13th thirteenth	30th thirtieth	1,000th one thousandth
4th fourth	14th fourteenth	40th fortieth	10,000th ten thousandth
5th fifth	15th fifteenth	50th fiftieth	100,000th one hundred thousandth
6th sixth	16th sixteenth	60th sixtieth	1,000,000th one millionth
7th seventh	17th seventeenth	70th seventieth	1,000,000,000th one billionth
8th eighth	18th eighteenth	80th eightieth	
9th ninth	19th nineteenth	90th ninetieth	
10th tenth	20th twentieth	100th one hundredth	

A. What floor do you live on?
B. I live on the _____ floor.

A. Is this your first trip to our country?
B. No. It's my _____ trip.

How many students are there in your class?

How many people are there in your country?

What were the names of your teachers in elementary school?
(My *first*-grade teacher was Ms./Mrs./Mr. . . .)

LÈ

two o'clock

two fifteen/
a quarter after *two*

two thirty/
half past *two*

two forty-five
a quarter to *three*

two oh five

two twenty/
twenty after *two*

two forty/
twenty to *three*

two fifty-five
five to *three*

A. What time is it?
B. It's _____.

A. What time does the movie
   begin?
B. At _____.

two A.M.

two P.M.

noon/
twelve noon

midnight/
twelve midnight

A. When does the train leave?
B. At _____.

A. What time will we arrive?
B. At _____.

Tell about your daily schedule:
   What do you do? When?
   (I get up at _____. I ....)

Do you usually have enough time to do
things, or do you "run out of time"?
Tell about it.

Tell about the use of time in different cultures or countries you know:
   Do people arrive on time for work? appointments? parties?
   Do trains and buses operate exactly on schedule?
   Do movies and sports events begin on time?
   Do workplaces use time clocks or timesheets to record employees' work hours?

LAJAN

Coins Pyès Lajan

Name	Value	Written as:	
1 penny	one cent	1¢	$ .01
2 nickel	five cents	5¢	$ .05
3 dime	ten cents	10¢	$ .10
4 quarter	twenty-five cents	25¢	$ .25
5 half dollar	fifty cents	50¢	$ .50
6 silver dollar	one dollar		$1.00

A. How much is a **penny** worth?
B. A **penny** is worth **one cent**.

A. *Soda* costs *ninety-five cents*. Do you have enough change?
B. Yes. I have a/two/three _____(s) and . . . .

Currency Papye Lajan

Name	We sometimes say:	Value	Written as:
7 (one-) dollar bill	a one	one dollar	$ 1.00
8 five-dollar bill	a five	five dollars	$ 5.00
9 ten-dollar bill	a ten	ten dollars	$ 10.00
10 twenty-dollar bill	a twenty	twenty dollars	$ 20.00
11 fifty-dollar bill	a fifty	fifty dollars	$ 50.00
12 (one-) hundred dollar bill	a hundred	one hundred dollars	$100.00

A. I'm going to the supermarket. Do you have any cash?
B. I have a **twenty-dollar bill**.
A. **Twenty dollars** is enough. Thanks.

A. Can you change a **five-dollar bill/a five**?
B. Yes. I have **five one-dollar bills/ five ones.**

Written as:	We say:
$1.30	a dollar and thirty cents
	a dollar thirty
$2.50	two dollars and fifty cents
	two fifty
$56.49	fifty-six dollars and forty-nine cents
	fifty-six forty-nine

Tell about some things you usually buy. What do they cost?

Name and describe the coins and currency in your country. What are they worth in U.S. dollars?

ALMANNAK LA

	anne	**1**	year
mwa		**2**	month
semèn/senmenn		**3**	week
jou		**4**	day
wikenn		**5**	weekend

Jou Semèn yo / Days of the Week

dimanch	**6**	Sunday
lendi	**7**	Monday
madi	**8**	Tuesday
mèkredi	**9**	Wednesday
jedi	**10**	Thursday
vandredi	**11**	Friday
samdi	**12**	Saturday

Mwa nan Anne yo / Months of the Year

janvye	**13**	January
fevriye	**14**	February
mas	**15**	March
avril	**16**	April
me	**17**	May
jen	**18**	June
jiyè	**19**	July
out	**20**	August
septanm	**21**	September
òktòb	**22**	October
novanm	**23**	November
desanm	**24**	December

3 janvye 2012	**25**	January 3, 2012
twa janvye de mil douz		January third, two thousand twelve
fèt	**26**	birthday
anivèsè	**27**	anniversary
randevou	**28**	appointment

A. What year is it?
B. It's _____.

[13–24]
A. What month is it?
B. It's _____.

[6–12]
A. What day is it?
B. It's _____.

A. What's today's date?
B. It's _____.

[26–28]
A. When is your _____?
B. It's on _____.

Which days of the week do you go to work/school?
(I go to work/school on _____.)

What do you do on the weekend?

What is your date of birth?
(I was born on ...... *month day, year* ......)

What's your favorite day of the week? Why?

What's your favorite month of the year? Why?

EKSPRESYON LÈ AK SEZON

	yè	**1**	yesterday
	jodiya	**2**	today
	demen	**3**	tomorrow
	maten	**4**	morning
	apremidi	**5**	afternoon
	aswè	**6**	evening
	lannuit	**7**	night
	yè maten	**8**	yesterday morning
	yè apremidi	**9**	yesterday afternoon
	yè swa	**10**	yesterday evening

	yè swa	**11**	last night
	maten an	**12**	this morning
	apremidi a	**13**	this afternoon
	aswè a	**14**	this evening
	aswè a	**15**	tonight
	demen maten	**16**	tomorrow morning
	demen apremidi	**17**	tomorrow afternoon
	demen swa	**18**	tomorrow evening
	demen swa	**19**	tomorrow night
	semenn pase	**20**	last week

	semenn sa a	**21**	this week
	semenn pwochenn	**22**	next week
	yon fwa pa semenn	**23**	once a week
	de fwa pa semenn	**24**	twice a week
	twa fwa pa semenn	**25**	three times a week
	chak jou	**26**	every day

Sezon Yo Seasons

	prentan	**27**	spring
	lete	**28**	summer
	lotòn	**29**	fall/autumn
	livè	**30**	winter

What did you do yesterday morning/afternoon/evening? What did you do last night?

What are you going to do tomorrow morning/afternoon/evening/night?

What did you do last week?

What are your plans for next week?

How many times a week do you have English class?/go to the supermarket?/exercise?

What's your favorite season? Why?

KALITE LOJMAN AK KOMINOTE YO

bilding ak apatman	**1**	apartment building	abri/kay pwovizwa	**9**	shelter
kay	**2**	house	fèm	**10**	farm
kay an 2 apatman	**3**	duplex/two-family house	ranch	**11**	ranch
kay kole	**4**	townhouse/townhome	kaybato	**12**	houseboat
kondo	**5**	condominium/condo	vil la	**13**	the city
dòtwa	**6**	dormitory/dorm	zòn andeyò lavil	**14**	the suburbs
trelè	**7**	mobile home	peyi a	**15**	the country
pansyon pou granmoun	**8**	nursing home	ti vil/vilaj	**16**	a town/village

A. Where do you live?

B. I live
- in a/an _____ [1–9] .
- on a _____ [10–12] .
- in _____ [13–16] .

[1–12]

A. Town Taxi Company.
B. Hello. Please send a taxi to
.....(address).....
A. Is that a house or an apartment building?
B. It's a/an _____.
A. All right. We'll be there right away.

[1–12]

A. This is the Emergency Operator.
B. Please send an ambulance to
.....(address).....
A. Is that a private home?
B. It's a/an _____.
A. What's your name and telephone number?
B. ....

Tell about people you know and where they live.

Discuss:
- Who lives in dormitories?
- Who lives in nursing homes?
- Who lives in shelters?
- Why?

SALON AN

etajè liv	**1**	bookcase	mi **10** wall	sofa/kannape **20** sofa/couch
pòtre/foto	**2**	picture/photograph	plafon **11** ceiling	plant **21** plant
tablo	**3**	painting	rido **12** drapes	tab salon **22** coffee table
tab chemine	**4**	mantel	fennèt **13** window	tapi **23** rug
chemine	**5**	fireplace	sofa 2 plas **14** loveseat	lanp **24** lamp
ekran chemine	**6**	fireplace screen	zòn anmizman **15** wall unit	abajou **25** lampshade
aparèy DVD	**7**	DVD player	wopalè **16** speaker	tab lanp **26** end table
televizyon	**8**	television/TV	aparèy estereyo **17** stereo system	planche **27** floor
VCR/anrejistrè kasètvideyo	**9**	VCR/video cassette recorder	mèb pou **18** magazine holder kenbe magazin	lanp kanpe atè **28** floor lamp
			zòrye/kousen **19** (throw) pillow	fotèy **29** armchair

A. Where are you?
B. I'm in the living room.
A. What are you doing?
B. I'm dusting* the **bookcase**.

* dusting/cleaning

A. You have a very nice living room!
B. Thank you.
A. Your _____ is/are beautiful!
B. Thank you for saying so.

A. Uh-oh! I just spilled coffee on your _____!
B. That's okay. Don't worry about it.

Tell about your living room.
(In my living room there's ....)

SALAMANJE A

tab salamanje	1	(dining room) table	vesèl pòslèn	12	china	nap	23	tablecloth
chèz salamanje	2	(dining room) chair	bòl salad	13	salad bowl	sèvyèt tab	24	napkin
pàntyè/gadmanje	3	buffet	bòl sèvis	14	serving bowl	fouchèt	25	fork
kabare	4	tray	asyèt pou sèvi	15	serving dish	asyèt	26	plate
teyè	5	teapot	po flè	16	vase	kouto	27	knife
kaftyè	6	coffee pot	bouji	17	candle	kiyè	28	spoon
sikriye	7	sugar bowl	pòtbouji	18	candlestick	bòl	29	bowl
pòtkrèm	8	creamer	plat	19	platter	gode	30	mug
po/podlo/pòtao	9	pitcher	berye	20	butter dish	vè	31	glass
chandelye	10	chandelier	salyè	21	salt shaker	tas	32	cup
veselye	11	china cabinet	pwavriye	22	pepper shaker	soukoup	33	saucer

A. This **dining room table** is very nice.
B. Thank you. It was a gift from my *grandmother*.*

*grandmother/grandfather/aunt/uncle/. . .

[In a store]
A. May I help you?
B. Yes, please. Do you have _____s?*
A. Yes. _____s* are right over there.
B. Thank you.

*With 12, use the singular

[At home]
A. Look at this old _____ I just bought!
B. Where did you buy it?
A. At a yard sale. How do you like it?
B. It's VERY unusual!

Tell about your dining room.
(In my dining room there's
..............)

CHANMAKOUCHE A

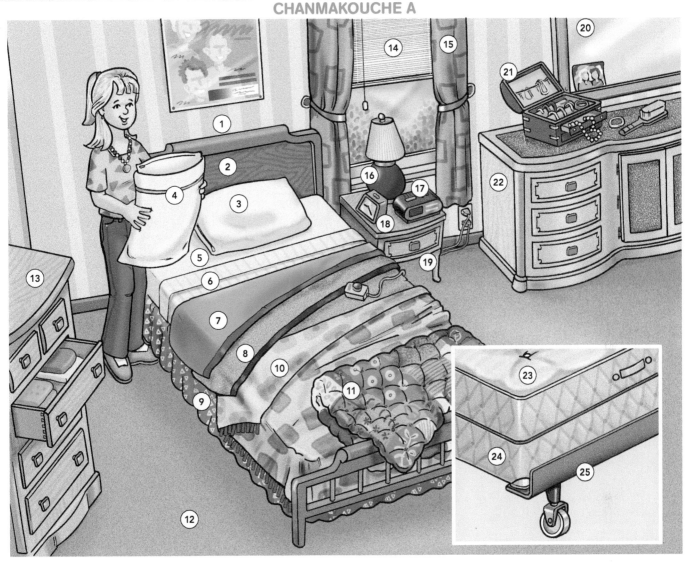

kabann	**1**	bed	jipon kabann	**9**	dust ruffle	radyo revèy	**18**	clock radio
tèt kabann	**2**	headboard	kouvreli	**10**	bedspread	tab dennwit	**19**	night table/
zòrye	**3**	pillow	kouvreli matlase	**11**	comforter/quilt			nightstand
tèdoreye	**4**	pillowcase	tapi	**12**	carpet	glas/miwa	**20**	mirror
dra ak elastik/	**5**	fitted sheet	komòd	**13**	chest (of drawers)	bwat bijou	**21**	jewelry box
dra fouwo			pèsyèn	**14**	blinds	kwafèz	**22**	dresser/bureau
dra	**6**	(flat) sheet	rido	**15**	curtains	matla	**23**	mattress
lenn	**7**	blanket	lanp	**16**	lamp	matla ak resò	**24**	box spring
lenn elektrik	**8**	electric blanket	revèy	**17**	alarm clock	kare kabann	**25**	bed frame

A. Ooh! Look at that big bug!
B. Where?
A. It's on the **bed**!
B. I'LL get it.

[In a store]

A. Excuse me. I'm looking for
a/an _____.*

B. We have some very nice _____s,
and they're all on sale this week!

A. Oh, good!

* With 14 & 15, use: Excuse me. I'm looking for _____

[In a bedroom]

A. Oh, no! I just lost my
contact lens!

B. Where?

A. I think it's on the _____.

B. I'll help you look.

Tell about your bedroom.
(In my bedroom there's ....)

Haitian	#	English
frijidè	1	refrigerator
frizè	2	freezer
poubèl/bwat fatra	3	garbage pail
batèz elektrik	4	(electric) mixer
plaka	5	cabinet
sipò tòchon papye	6	paper towel holder
kànistè	7	canister
kontwa kuizin	8	(kitchen) counter
savon vesèl	9	dishwasher
an poud		detergent
savon vesèl likid	10	dishwashing liquid
wobinèt/tiyo	11	faucet
evye	12	(kitchen) sink
machin vesèl	13	dishwasher

Haitian	#	English
moulen dechè	14	(garbage) disposal
tòchon vesèl	15	dish towel
panyen asyèt	16	dish rack/
		dish drainer
etajè epis	17	spice rack
ouvbwat eletrik	18	(electric) can
		opener
blenndè	19	blender
fou po griye/	20	toaster oven
fou tostè		
mikwowev	21	microwave (oven)
tòchon chodyè	22	potholder
kafetyè pou te	23	tea kettle
founo	24	stove/range

Haitian	#	English
recho	25	burner
fou	26	oven
tostè	27	toaster
kafetyè	28	coffeemaker
konpresè	29	trash
fatra		compactor
planchèt pou	30	cutting
dekoupe		board
liv kwizin	31	cookbook
aparèy moulen	32	food
manje		processor
chèz kwizin	33	kitchen chair
tab kwizin	34	kitchen table
napwon	35	placemat

A. I think we need a new **refrigerator**.
B. I think you're right.

[In a store]

A. Excuse me. Are your _____s still on sale?

B. Yes, they are. They're twenty percent off.

[In a kitchen]

A. When did you get this/these new _____(s)?

B. I got it/them last week.

Tell about your kitchen.
(In my kitchen there's ....)

nounous	1	teddy bear	poubèl pou	10	diaper pail	vwati bebe	21	baby carriage
monitè pou bebe/	2	baby monitor/	kouchèt			chèz bebe	22	car seat/
entèkòm		intercom	neyèz	11	night light	pou machin		safety seat
komòd	3	chest (of drawers)	bwat jwèt	12	toy chest	vwati bebe	23	baby carrier
bèso/kabann bebe	4	crib	jwèt boure	13	stuffed animal	asyèt bebe	24	food warmer
pwotèj bèso	5	crib bumper/	pope	14	doll	chèz pou wose bebe	25	booster seat
		bumper pad	balanswa	15	swing	chèz bebe	26	baby seat
jwèt mobil	6	mobile	pak bebe	16	playpen	chèz wo pou bebe	27	high chair
tab pou chanje	7	changing table	tchatcha	17	rattle	bèso pliyan	28	portable crib
kouchèt			twotinèt	18	walker	vaz bebe	29	potty
salopèt bebe	8	stretch suit	bèso	19	cradle	sakavant pou bebe	30	baby frontpack
kousinyè pou	9	changing pad	pousèt bebe	20	stroller	sakado pou bebe	31	baby backpack
chanje bebe								

A. Thank you for the **teddy bear**. It's a very nice gift.
B. You're welcome. Tell me, when are you due?
A. In a few more weeks.

A. That's a very nice _____.
Where did you get it?

B. It was a gift from ....

A. Do you have everything you need
before the baby comes?

B. Almost everything. We're still
looking for a/an _____ and a/an
_____.

Tell about your country:
What things do people buy for a new baby?
Does a new baby sleep in a separate room,
as in the United States?

SALDEBEN AN

poubèl	**1**	wastebasket	sechwa cheve	**14**	hair dryer	santibon pou twalèt	**25**	air freshener

poubèl **1** wastebasket
bifèt twalèt **2** vanity
savon **3** soap
savonnye **4** soap dish
ponp savon likid **5** soap dispenser
lavabo **6** (bathroom) sink
wobinèt/tiyo **7** faucet
bifèt medikaman **8** medicine cabinet
glas/miwa **9** mirror
tas **10** cup
bwòsdan **11** toothbrush
sipò bwòsdan **12** toothbrush holder
bwòsdan elektrik **13** electric toothbrush

sechwa cheve **14** hair dryer
etajè **15** shelf
panyen rad sal **16** hamper
vantilatè **17** fan
sèvyèt deben **18** bath towel
sèvyèt men **19** hand towel
sèvyèt twalèt **20** washcloth/ faceloth
pòtsèvyèt **21** towel rack
ponp watè **22** plunger
bwòs twalèt **23** toilet brush
papye ijyenik **24** toilet paper

santibon pou twalèt **25** air freshener
watè **26** toilet
rebò watè **27** toilet seat
douch **28** shower
wobinèt douch **29** shower head
rido douch **30** shower curtain
benywa/basen **31** bathtub/tub
tapi kawotchou **32** rubber mat
tiyo drennaj **33** drain
eponj **34** sponge
tapi saldeben **35** bath mat
balans **36** scale

A. Where's the **hair dryer**?
B. It's *on* the **vanity**.

A. Where's the **soap**?
B. It's *in* the **soap dish**.

A. Where's the **plunger**?
B. It's *next to* the **toilet brush**.

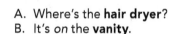

A. [Knock. Knock.] Did I leave my glasses in there?
B. Yes. They're on/in/next to the _____.

A. *Bobby*? You didn't clean up the bathroom! There's toothpaste on the _____, and there's powder all over the _____!
B. Sorry. I'll clean it up right away.

Tell about your bathroom.
(In my bathroom there's ....)

DEYÒ KAY LA

Lakou Devan	**Front Yard**		pèsyèn	**12**	shutter	teras an bwa	**23** deck
poto limyè	**1** lamppost		twati/dokay	**13**	roof	recho griyad	**24** barbecue/
bwat lapòs	**2** mailbox		garaj	**14**	garage		(outdoor) grill
ale devan	**3** front walk		pòt garaj	**15**	garage door	pasyo	**25** patio
eskalye devan	**4** front steps		ale garaj	**16**	driveway	goutyè	**26** gutter
galri devan kay	**5** (front) porch					tiyo goutyè	**27** drainpipe
pòt siklòn	**6** storm door		**Lakou Dèyè**	**Backyard**		antèn parabolik	**28** satellite dish
pòt devan	**7** front door		chèz long/gazon	**17**	lawn chair	antèn	**29** TV antenna
sonnèt	**8** doorbell		tondèz gazon	**18**	lawnmower	chemine	**30** chimney
limyè devan	**9** (front) light		depo zouti	**19**	tool shed	pòt sou kote	**31** side door
fennèt	**10** window		pòt til	**20**	screen door	kloti	**32** fence
til nan fennèt	**11** (window) screen		pòt dèyè	**21**	back door		
			manch pòt	**22**	door knob		

A. When are you going to repair the **lamppost**?
B. I'm going to repair it next Saturday.

[On the telephone]
A. Harry's Home Repairs.
B. Hello. Do you fix _____s?
A. No, we don't.
B. Oh, okay. Thank you.

[At work on Monday morning]
A. What did you do this weekend?
B. Nothing much. I repaired my _____ and my _____.

Do you like to repair things?
What things can you repair yourself?
What things can't you repair? Who repairs them?

BILDING AK APATMAN

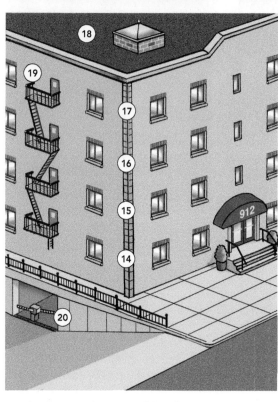

Sèche apatman	**Looking for an Apartment**
seksyon reklam apatman/nan jounal	**1** apartment ads/ classified ads
lis apatman ki nan piblisite	**2** apartment listings
siy kay ki vid	**3** vacancy sign

Siyen yon kontra	**Signing a Lease**
lokatè	**4** tenant
mèt kay la	**5** landlord
kontra	**6** lease
depo	**7** security deposit

Pran lojman	**Moving In**
kamyon kap bwote	**8** moving truck/ moving van
vwazen	**9** neighbor
jeran	**10** building manager
jeran baryè	**11** doorman
kle	**12** key
seri	**13** lock
premye etaj	**14** first floor
dezyèm etaj	**15** second floor
twazyèm etaj	**16** third floor
katriyèm etaj	**17** fourth floor
twati/dokay	**18** roof

eskalye ijans	**19**	fire escape
garaj	**20**	parking garage
balkon	**21**	balcony
lakou	**22**	courtyard
pakin	**23**	parking lot
plas pakin	**24**	parking space
pisin	**25**	swimming pool
basen dlo souke	**26**	whirlpool
panye fatra	**27**	trash bin
klimatizè	**28**	air conditioner

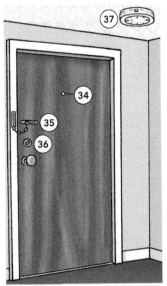

Antre Lobby		**Koulwa Hallway**		**Besment Basement**	
entèkòm	**29** intercom/speaker	ekzit pou	**38** fire exit/	depo	**43** storage room
sonnèt	**30** buzzer	epanye dife/	emergency stairway	kazye	**44** storage locker
bwat lapòs	**31** mailbox	eskalye ijan		sal lesiv	**45** laundry room
elevatè	**32** elevator	alam dife	**39** fire alarm	baryè sekirite	**46** security gate
eskalye	**33** stairway	sistèm awozaj	**40** sprinkler system		
		jeran	**41** superintendent		
Pòt Dantre Doorway		twou fatra	**42** garbage chute/		
pòt ak twou jouda	**34** peephole		trash chute		
chenn pòt	**35** (door) chain				
seri	**36** dead-bolt lock				
alam pou lafimen	**37** smoke detector				

[19–46]
A. Is there a **fire escape**?
B. Yes, there is. Do you want to see the apartment?
A. Yes, I do.

[19–46]

[Renting an apartment]
A. Let me show you around.
B. Okay.
A. This is the _____, and here's the _____.
B. I see.

[19–46]

[On the telephone]
A. Mom and Dad? I found an apartment.
B. Good. Tell us about it.
A. It has a/an _____ and a/an _____.
B. That's nice. Does it have a/an _____?
A. Yes, it does.

Do you or someone you know live in an apartment building? Tell about it.

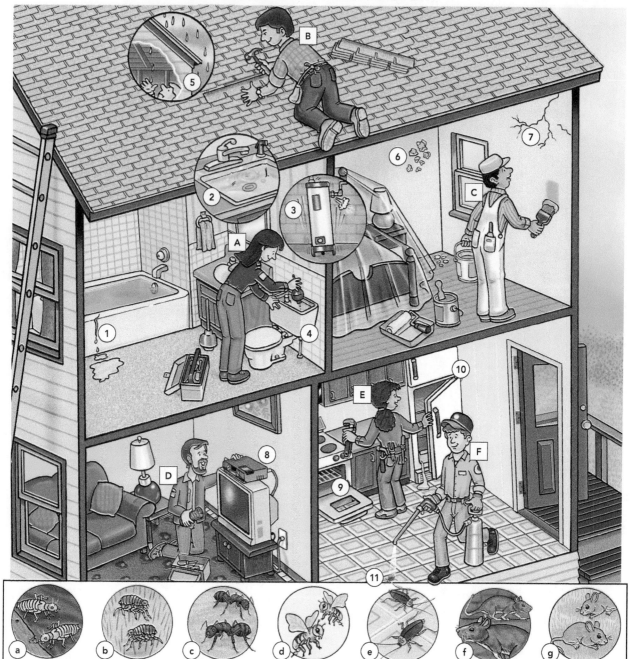

plonbye	**A**	**plumber**
Benywa ap koule.	**1**	The bathtub is leaking.
Lavabo a bouche.	**2**	The sink is clogged.
Dlo cho a pap travay.	**3**	The hot water heater isn't working.
Twalèt la kraze.	**4**	The toilet is broken.
bòs twati	**B**	**roofer**
Do kay la koule.	**5**	The roof is leaking.
(kay) pent	**C**	**(house) painter**
Penti a ap dekale.	**6**	The paint is peeling.
Mi an fann/pete.	**7**	The wall is cracked.
konpanyi pou televizyon	**D**	**cable TV company**
Kab televizyon an pap travay.	**8**	The cable TV isn't working.

bòs tout metye	**E**	**appliance repairperson**
Fou a pap travay.	**9**	The stove isn't working.
Frijidè a kraze.	**10**	The refrigerator is broken.
ekstèminatè	**F**	**exterminator / pest control specialist**
Geneyn ____ nan kizin/kuizin nan.	**11**	There are ____ in the kitchen.
foumi bwa		**a** termites
pis		**b** fleas
foumi		**c** ants
myèl		**d** bees
ravèt		**e** cockroaches
rat		**f** rats
sourit		**g** mice

| serirye | **G locksmith** |
| Seri a kraze. | **12** The lock is broken. |

elektrisyen	**H electrician**
Limyè devan an pa limen.	**13** The front light doesn't go on.
Sonèt la pa travay.	**14** The doorbell doesn't ring.
Pa gen kouran nan salon an.	**15** The power is out in the living room.

| netwayè chemine | **I chimneysweep** |
| Chemine a sal. | **16** The chimney is dirty. |

| bòs tout metye | **J home repairperson/"handyman"** |
| Mozayik nan twalèt la sekwe. | **17** The tiles in the bathroom are loose. |

chapantye	**K carpenter**
Eskalye yo kraze.	**18** The steps are broken.
Pòt la pa louvri.	**19** The door doesn't open.

sèvis chofaj ak è kondisyone	**L heating and air conditioning service**
Chalè nan sistèm nan p ap mache.	**20** The heating system is broken.
Èkondisyone a p ap travay.	**21** The air conditioning isn't working.

A. What's the matter?
B. ___[1–21]___.
A. I think we should call a/an ___[A–L]___.

[1–21]

A. I'm having a problem in my apartment/house.
B. What's the problem?
A. _____.

[A–L]

A. Can you recommend a good _____?
B. Yes. You should call ....

What do you do when there are problems in your home? Do you fix things yourself, or do you call someone?

NETWAYE KAY OU

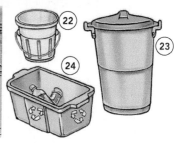

bale atè a	**A**	sweep the floor
pase vakyòm	**B**	vacuum
mòp atè a	**C**	mop the floor
lave fennèt yo	**D**	wash the windows
siye	**E**	dust
sire atè a	**F**	wax the floor
poli mèb yo	**G**	polish the furniture
netwaye	**H**	clean the bathroom
saldeben an		
mete fatra a deyò	**I**	take out the garbage

bale	**1**	broom
ranmaswa	**2**	dustpan
epousèt	**3**	whisk broom

bale pou tapi	**4**	carpet sweeper
vakyòm/aspirate	**5**	vacuum (cleaner)
pyès pou aspiratè	**6**	vacuum cleaner attachments
sak vakyòm	**7**	vacuum cleaner bag
vakyòm ak men	**8**	hand vacuum
mòp pou netwaye pousyè/mòp seche	**9**	(dust) mop/ (dry) mop
mòp eponj	**10**	(sponge) mop
mòp mouye	**11**	(wet) mop
tòchon papye	**12**	paper towels
likid pou netwaye fennèt	**13**	window cleaner

amonyak	**14**	ammonia
twal epouste/ chifon	**15**	dust cloth
bale an plim	**16**	feather duster
likid pou sire planch	**17**	floor wax
poli pou mèb	**18**	furniture polish
bagay pou netwaye	**19**	cleanser
bwòs netwayaj	**20**	scrub brush
eponj	**21**	sponge
bokit	**22**	bucket/pail
bwat fatra	**23**	trash can/ garbage can
kès pou bwat fèblan	**24**	recycling bin

[A–I]
A. What are you doing?
B. I'm **sweep**ing **the floor.**

[1–24]
A. I can't find the **broom**.
B. Look over there!

[1–12, 15, 16, 20–24]
A. Excuse me. Do you sell _____(s)?
B. Yes. They're at the back of the store.
A. Thanks.

[13, 14, 17–19]
A. Excuse me. Do you sell _____?
B. Yes. It's at the back of the store.
A. Thanks.

What household cleaning chores do people do in your home? What things do they use?

BAGAY POU KAY

yad an bwa	**1**	yardstick	tep mens elastik	**11**	duct tape	papye sable	**20** sandpaper
chasmouch	**2**	fly swatter	pil	**12**	batteries	penti	**21** paint
ponp	**3**	plunger	anpoul elektrik	**13**	lightbulbs/bulbs	tine	**22** paint thinner
flach	**4**	flashlight	fizib	**14**	fuses	penso	**23** paintbrush/brush
ralonj elektrik	**5**	extension cord	lwil motè/luil motè	**15**	oil	plato penti	**24** paint pan
mèt	**6**	tape measure	lakòl	**16**	glue	woulo pou penti	**25** paint roller
nechèl	**7**	step ladder	gan travay	**17**	work gloves	flit	**26** spray gun
sourisye	**8**	mousetrap	ensèktisid	**18**	bug spray/insect spray		
tep papye	**9**	masking tape	destriktè ravèt	**19**	roach killer		
tep elektrik	**10**	electrical tape					

A. I can't find the **yardstick**!
B. Look in the utility cabinet.
A. I did.
B. Oh! Wait a minute! I lent the **yardstick** to the neighbors.

[1–8, 23–26]

A. I'm going to the hardware store. Can you think of anything we need?

B. Yes. We need a/an _____.

A. Oh, that's right.

[9–22]

A. I'm going to the hardware store. Can you think of anything we need?

B. Yes. We need _____.

A. Oh, that's right.

What home supplies do you have? How and when do you use each one?

ZOUTI AK PYÈS

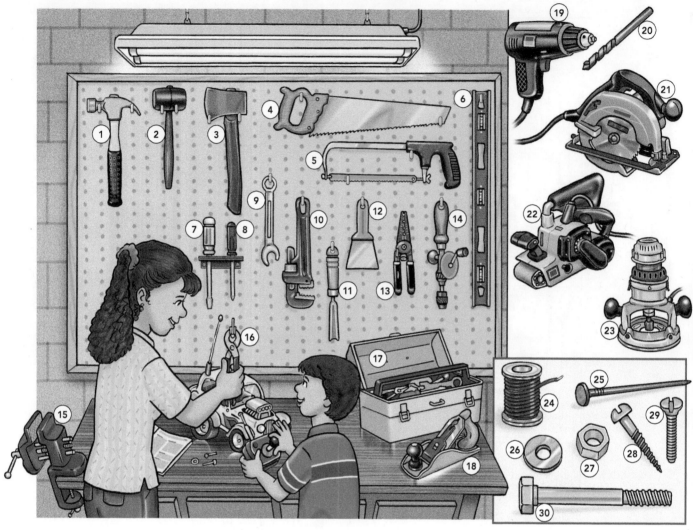

mato	**1** hammer	gratwa	**12** scraper	aparèy pou sab	**22** power sander
mayèt	**2** mallet	sizo pou fil elektrik	**13** wire stripper	elektrik	
hach/rach	**3** ax	dril	**14** hand drill	woutye	**23** router
si	**4** saw/handsaw	eto	**15** vise	fil elektrik	**24** wire
si ameto	**5** hacksaw	pens/tennay	**16** pliers	klou	**25** nail
nivo	**6** level	bwat zouti	**17** toolbox	wondèl	**26** washer
tounvis	**7** screwdriver	rabo	**18** plane	ekwou	**27** nut
tounvis zetwal	**8** Phillips screwdriver	dril elektrik	**19** electric drill	ekwou bwa	**28** wood screw
kle plat	**9** wrench	mèch	**20** (drill) bit	ekwou machin	**29** machine screw
kle tiyo	**10** monkey wrench/ pipe wrench	si elektrik	**21** circular saw/ power saw	boulon	**30** bolt
biren/sizo	**11** chisel				

A. Can I borrow your **hammer**?
B. Sure.
A. Thanks.

* With 25–30, use: Could I borrow some _____s?

[1–15, 17–24]
A. Where's the _____?
B. It's on/next to/near/over/under the _____.

[16, 25–30]
A. Where are the _____s?
B. They're on/next to/near/over/under the _____.

Do you like to work with tools?
What tools do you have in your home?

ZOUTI JADEN AK AKTIVITE

koupe zèb la	**A** mow the lawn	tondèz gazon	**1** lawnmower	awozwa otomatik	**12** sprinkler
plante legim	**B** plant vegetables	bidon gaz	**2** gas can	awozwa	**13** watering can
plante flè	**C** plant flowers	aparèy egalize gazon	**3** line trimmer	bale fè	**14** rake
awouze flè yo	**D** water the flowers	pèl	**4** shovel	vante fèy	**15** leaf blower
bale fèy yo	**E** rake leaves	semans legim	**5** vegetable seeds	sak plastik	**16** yard waste bag
koupe bòdi a	**F** trim the hedge	wou	**6** hoe	tondèz bòdi	**17** (hedge) clippers
koupe raje yo	**G** prune the bushes	tiwèl	**7** trowel	aparèy pou	**18** hedge trimmer
raje	**H** weed	bourèt	**8** wheelbarrow	koupe bòdi	
		angrè	**9** fertilizer	sekatè	**19** pruning shears
		tiyo awozaj	**10** (garden) hose	aparèy pou	**20** weeder
		bèk tiyo awozaj	**11** nozzle	koupe raje	

[A–H]
A. Hi! Are you busy?
B. Yes. I'm **mow**ing **the lawn**.

[1–20]
A. What are you looking for?
B. The **lawnmower**.

[A–H]
A. What are you going to do tomorrow?
B. I'm going to _____.

[1–20]
A. Can I borrow your _____?
B. Sure.

Do you ever work with any of these tools? Which ones? What do you do with them?

PLACES AROUND TOWN I

DIVÈS KOTE NAN LAVIL LA I

boulanjri	1	bakery	vandè machin/dilè	7	car dealership	magazen rad	12	clothing store
bank	2	bank	magazen kat	8	card store	magazen pou manje leje	13	coffee shop
kwafè	3	barber shop	gadri	9	child-care center / day-care center			
magazen liv	4	book store				magazen konpitè	14	computer store
estasyon bis	5	bus station	drayklining	10	cleaners / dry cleaners	boutik asòti	15	convenience store
magazen sirèt	6	candy store	klinik	11	clinic	sant polikopye	16	copy center

boutik sandwich ak konsèv	**17** delicatessen/deli	restoran manje prese	**24** fast-food restaurant
magazen varyete	**18** department store	magazen flè	**25** flower shop/florist
magazen bon mache	**19** discount store	magazen mèb	**26** furniture store
ba dounòt	**20** donut shop	estasyon	**27** gas station/
famasi	**21** drug store/pharmacy	gazolin	service station
magazen elektwonik	**22** electronics store	episri	**28** grocery store
sant pou swen zye	**23** eye-care center/optician		

A. Where are you going?
B. I'm going to the **bakery**.

A. Hi! How are you today?
B. Fine. Where are you going?
A. To the _____. How about you?
B. I'm going to the _____.

A. Oh, no! I can't find my wallet/purse!
B. Did you leave it at the _____?
A. Maybe I did.

Which of these places are in your neighborhood?
(In my neighborhood there's a/an ....)

DIVÈS KOTE NAN LAVIL LA II

salondbote	**1** hair salon	magazen bijou	**7** jewelry store
magazen kenkay	**2** hardware store	blanchisri otomatik	**8** laundromat
klib egzèsis	**3** health club	bibliyotèk	**9** library
lopital	**4** hospital	magazen fanm ansent	**10** maternity shop
otèl	**5** hotel	motèl	**11** motel
boutik krèmalaglas	**6** ice cream shop	sinema	**12** movie theater

magazen mizik	**13** music store	
estidyo maniki	**14** nail salon	
ak pediki		
pak	**15** park	
magazen atik	**16** pet shop/	
bèt kay		pet store

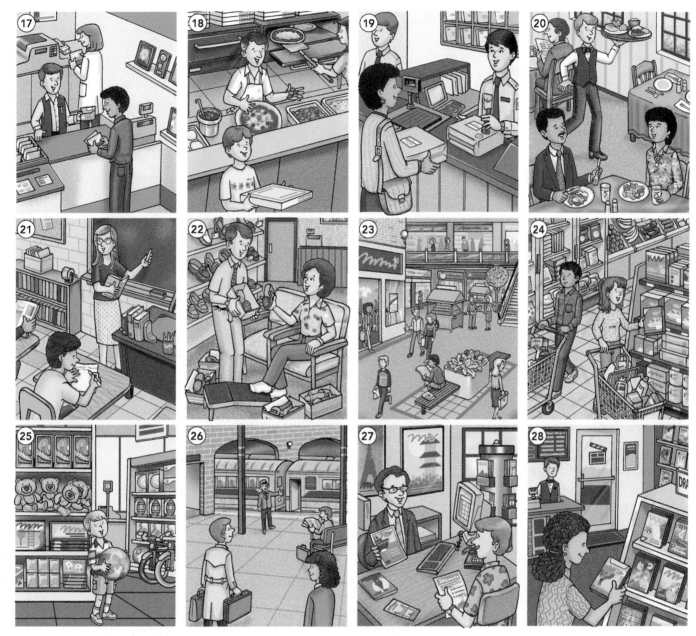

magazen foto	**17**	photo shop	lekòl	**21**	school	magazen jwèt	**25**	toy store
boutik pitza	**18**	pizza shop	magazen soulye	**22**	shoe store	estasyon tren	**26**	train station
lapòs	**19**	post office	sant komès	**23**	(shopping) mall	ajans vwayaj	**27**	travel agency
restoran	**20**	restaurant	sipèmakèt	**24**	supermarket	magazen videyo	**28**	video store

A. Where's the **hair salon**?
B. It's right over there.

A. Is there a/an _____ nearby?
B. Yes. There's a/an _____ around the corner.
A. Thanks.

A. Excuse me. Where's the _____?
B. It's down the street, next to the _____.
A. Thank you.

Which of these places are in your neighborhood?
(In my neighborhood there's a/an …………)

tribinal	**1**	courthouse	bwat sonnèt pou dife	**8**	fire alarm box
taksi/laliy	**2**	taxi/cab/taxicab	bwat postal/ bwat lèt	**9**	mailbox
estasyon taksi	**3**	taxi stand	devèswa egou	**10**	sewer
chofè taksi/ chofè laliy	**4**	taxi driver/ cab driver	estasyon polis	**11**	police station
tiyo ponpye	**5**	fire hydrant	prizon	**12**	jail
panyen fatra	**6**	trash container	twotwa	**13**	sidewalk
meri/lakomin	**7**	city hall			

lari	**14**	street
limyè lari	**15**	street light
plas pakin	**16**	parking lot
kontwolè kontè pakin	**17**	meter maid
kontè pakin	**18**	parking meter
kamyon fatra	**19**	garbage truck
sòbwe	**20**	subway
estasyon sòbwe	**21**	subway station

boutik jounal	**22**	newsstand	rebò twotwa	**29**	curb	telefòn piblik	**36** public telephone
limyè trafik	**23**	traffic light / traffic signal	pakin ann etaj	**30**	parking garage	ansèy lari	**37** street sign
kalfou	**24**	intersection	estasyon ponpye	**31**	fire station	twou egou	**38** manhole
ajan lapolis/jandam	**25**	police officer	estasyon bis	**32**	bus stop	motosiklèt	**39** motorcycle
pasaj pyeton	**26**	crosswalk	bis	**33**	bus	machann sou twotwa	**40** street vendor
pyeton	**27**	pedestrian	chofè bis	**34**	bus driver	gichè pou machin	**41** drive-through window
kamyon krèm	**28**	ice cream truck	bilding pou biwo	**35**	office building		

A. Where's the _____?
B. On/In/Next to/Between/Across from/ In front of/Behind/Under/Over the _____.

Go to an intersection in your city or town. What do you see? Make a list. Then tell about it.

[An Election Speech]

If I am elected mayor, I'll take care of all the problems in our city. We need to do something about our _____s. We also need to do something about our _____s. And look at our _____s! We REALLY need to do something about THEM! We need a new mayor who can solve these problems. If I am elected mayor, we'll be proud of our _____s, _____s, and _____s again! Vote for me!

MOUN AK DESKRIPSYON FIZIK

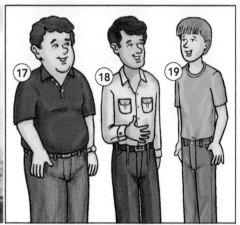

timoun-timoun yo	**1**	**child-children**
bebe	**2**	baby/infant
ti moun k ap aprann mache	**3**	toddler
gason	**4**	boy
fi	**5**	girl
jèn	**6**	teenager
granmoun	**7**	**adult**
gason-gason yo	**8**	man–men
fanm-fanm yo	**9**	woman–women
retrete	**10**	senior citizen/ elderly person

laj	**age**	
jenn	**11**	young
mwayen daj	**12**	middle-aged
vye	**13**	old/elderly
wotè	**height**	
wo	**14**	tall
wotè mwayenn	**15**	average height
kout	**16**	short
pwa	**weight**	
lou	**17**	heavy
pwa mwayenn	**18**	average weight
mèg	**19**	thin/slim
ansent	**20**	pregnant

enfim/ kokobe	**21**	physically challenged
wè twoub	**22**	vision impaired
moun ki tande di	**23**	hearing impaired

Dekri cheve		Describing Hair		nwa	30	black
long	24	long		mawon	31	brown
longè zepòl/	25	shoulder length		blon	32	blond
rive sou zepòl				wouj	33	red
kout	26	short		gri	34	gray
swa	27	straight		chòv	35	bald
boukle (cheve)	28	wavy				
boukle	29	curly		bab	36	beard
				moustach	37	mustache

A. Tell me about *your brother.*
B. *He's a tall heavy boy* with *short curly brown* hair.

A. What does *your new boss* look like?
B. *She's average height,* and *she* has *long straight black* hair.

A. Can you describe *the person*?
B. *He's a tall thin middle-aged man.*
A. Anything else?
B. Yes. *He's bald,* and *he* has *a mustache.*

A. Can you describe *your grandmother*?
B. *She's a short thin elderly person* with *long wavy gray* hair.
A. Anything else?
B. Yes. *She's hearing impaired.*

Tell about yourself.

Tell about people in your family.

Tell about your favorite actor or actress or other famous person.

DESKRIPSYON MOUN AK BAGAY

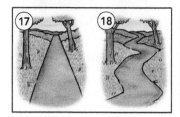

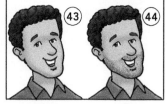

nèf/nouvo – vye	1–2 new – old	fonse – klè	25–26 dark – light
jenn – vye	3–4 young – old	wo – ba	27–28 high – low
wo – kout	5–6 tall – short	lach – sere	29–30 loose – tight
long – kout	7–8 long – short	bon – move	31–32 good – bad
gwo – ti/piti	9–10 large/big – small/little	cho – frèt	33–34 hot – cold
rapid – dousman	11–12 fast – slow	annòd – andezòd	35–36 neat – messy
lou/gra – mèg/chèch	13–14 heavy/fat – thin/skinny	pwòp – sal	37–38 clean – dirty
lou – lejè	15–16 heavy – light	mou – di	39–40 soft – hard
dwa – kwochi	17–18 straight – crooked	fasil – difisil/di	41–42 easy – difficult/hard
swa – boukle	19–20 straight – curly	vlou – graj	43–44 smooth – rough
laj – etwat	21–22 wide – narrow	gwo bwi/eskandal – trankil/pezib	45–46 noisy/loud – quiet
pwès – mens	23–24 thick – thin	marye – selibatè	47–48 married – single

rich – pòv	**49–50** rich/wealthy – poor	bòzò – senp	**63–64** fancy – plain
bèl – lèd	**51–52** pretty/beautiful – ugly	klere – mat	**65–66** shiny – dull
bèl gason – lèd	**53–54** handsome – ugly	file – pa file	**67–68** sharp – dull
mouye – sèk	**55–56** wet – dry	alèz – pa alèz	**69–70** comfortable – uncomfortable
louvri – fèmen	**57–58** open – closed		
plen – vid	**59–60** full – empty	onèt – malonèt	**71–72** honest – dishonest
chè – bon mache	**61–62** expensive – cheap/inexpensive		

[1–2]
A. Is your car **new**?
B. No. It's **old**.

1–2	Is your car _____?	25–26	Is the room _____?	49–50	Is your uncle _____?
3–4	Is he _____?	27–28	Is the bridge _____?	51–52	Is the witch _____?
5–6	Is your sister _____?	29–30	Are the pants _____?	53–54	Is the pirate _____?
7–8	Is his hair _____?	31–32	Are your neighbor's children _____?	55–56	Are the clothes _____?
9–10	Is their dog _____?	33–34	Is the water _____?	57–58	Is the door _____?
11–12	Is the train _____?	35–36	Is your desk _____?	59–60	Is the pitcher _____?
13–14	Is your friend _____?	37–38	Are the windows _____?	61–62	Is that restaurant _____?
15–16	Is the box _____?	39–40	Is the mattress _____?	63–64	Is the dress _____?
17–18	Is the road _____?	41–42	Is the homework _____?	65–66	Is your kitchen floor _____?
19–20	Is her hair _____?	43–44	Is your skin _____?	67–68	Is the knife _____?
21–22	Is the tie _____?	45–46	Is your neighbor _____?	69–70	Is the chair _____?
23–24	Is the line _____?	47–48	Is your sister _____?	71–72	Is he _____?

A. Tell me about your ....
B. He's/She's/It's/They're _____.

A. Do you have a/an _____ ....?
B. No. I have a/an _____ ....

Describe yourself.

Describe a person you know.

Describe some things in your home.

Describe some things in your community.

DESCRIBING PHYSICAL STATES AND EMOTIONS

DESKRIPSYON KONDISYON FIZIK AK SANTIMAN

bouke	**1**	tired
dòmi nanje	**2**	sleepy
bouke anpil	**3**	exhausted
malad	**4**	sick / ill
cho	**5**	hot
frèt	**6**	cold
grangou	**7**	hungry
swaf	**8**	thirsty
plen	**9**	full
kontan	**10**	happy
tris/kè pa kontan	**11**	sad / unhappy
mizerab	**12**	miserable
eksite	**13**	excited
kontraye	**14**	disappointed
vèkse	**15**	upset
annwiye	**16**	annoyed

move	**17** angry/mad	sèl	**23** lonely
debòde/dechennen	**18** furious	nostaljik	**24** homesick
degoute	**19** disgusted	annève	**25** nervous
fache	**20** frustrated	enkyete	**26** worried
sezi	**21** surprised	pè/lapè	**27** scared/afraid
choke	**22** shocked	anbete	**28** bored

fyè	**29** proud
jennen	**30** embarrassed
jalou	**31** jealous
bwouye	**32** confused

A. You look _____.
B. I am. I'm VERY _____.

A. Are you _____?
B. No. Why do you ask? Do I LOOK _____?
A. Yes. You do.

What makes you happy? sad? mad?

What do you do when you feel nervous? annoyed?

Do you ever feel embarrassed? When?

FWI

pòm **1** apple	fig frans **12** fig	zoranj **22** orange
pèch **2** peach	kokoye **13** coconut	mandarin **23** tangerine
pwa **3** pear	zaboka **14** avocado	rezen **24** grapes
fig **4** banana	kantaloup **15** cantaloupe	seriz **25** cherries
bannann **5** plantain	melon **16** honeydew	prin seche **26** prunes
prin **6** plum	myèl (melon)	dat **27** dates
zabriko **7** apricot	melon dlo **17** watermelon	rezen sèk **28** raisins
nektarin **8** nectarine	zannanna **18** pineapple	nwa **29** nuts
kiwi **9** kiwi	chadèk **19** grapefruit	franbwaz **30** raspberries
papay **10** papaya	sitwon jòn **20** lemon	blouberi **31** blueberries
mango **11** mango	sitwon vèt **21** lime	frèz **32** strawberries

[1–23]
A. This **apple** is delicious! Where did you get it?
B. At *Sam's Supermarket*.

[24–32]
A. These **grapes** are delicious! Where did you get them?
B. At *Franny's Fruit Stand*.

A. I'm hungry. Do we have any fruit?
B. Yes. We have _____s* and _____s.*

A. Do we have any more _____s?†
B. No. I'll get some more when I go to the supermarket.

*With 15–19, use:
  We have _____ and _____.

†With 15–19 use:
  Do we have any more _____?

What are your favorite fruits?
Which fruits don't you like?

Which of these fruits grow where you live?

Name and describe other fruits you know.

LEGIM

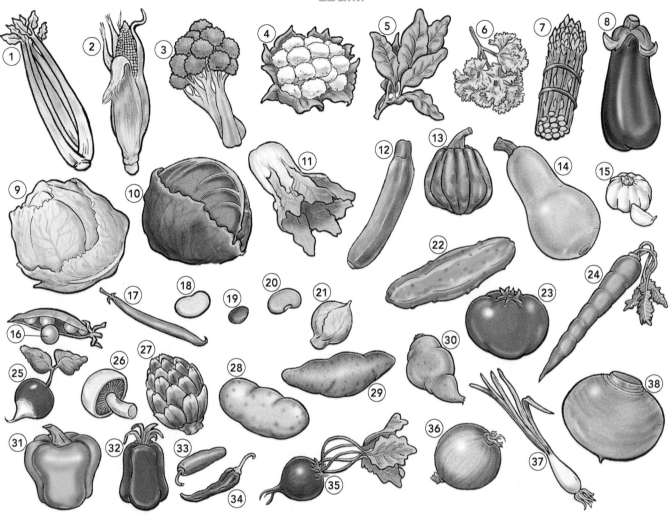

seleri	**1**	celery
mayi	**2**	corn
bwokoli	**3**	broccoli
chouflè	**4**	cauliflower
zepina	**5**	spinach
pèsi	**6**	parsley
aspèj	**7**	asparagus
obèjin/berejenn	**8**	eggplant
leti	**9**	lettuce
chou	**10**	cabbage
bòk chòy	**11**	bok choy
eskwach	**12**	zucchini
jouwoumou	**13**	acorn squash
jouwoumou po jòn	**14**	butternut squash

lay	**15**	garlic
pwa nwa	**16**	pea
pwatann	**17**	string bean/green bean
pwadsouch	**18**	lima bean
pwa nwa	**19**	black bean
pwa enkòni	**20**	kidney bean
chou briksèl	**21**	brussels sprout
konkonm	**22**	cucumber
tonmat	**23**	tomato
kawòt	**24**	carrot
radi	**25**	radish
djondjon/chanpiyon	**26**	mushroom
aticho	**27**	artichoke

ponmtè	**28**	potato
patat	**29**	sweet potato
patat jòn/yanm	**30**	yam
piman dous vèt	**31**	green pepper/sweet pepper
piman dous wouj	**32**	red pepper
piman zwazo vèt	**33**	jalapeño (pepper)
piman zwazo wouj	**34**	chili pepper
bètwouj	**35**	beet
zonyon	**36**	onion
siv	**37**	scallion/green onion
nave	**38**	turnip

A. What do we need from the supermarket?
B. We need **celery*** and **peas**.†

* 1–15　　　† 16–38

A. How do you like the ___[1–15]___ / ___[16–38]___s?
B. It's/They're delicious.

A. *Bobby*? Finish your vegetables!
B. But you KNOW I hate ___[1–15]___ / ___[16–38]___s!
A. I know. But it's/they're good for you!

Which vegetables do you like?
Which vegetables don't you like?

Which of these vegetables grow where you live?

Name and describe other vegetables you know.

VYANN, VOLAY AK MANJE LANMÈ

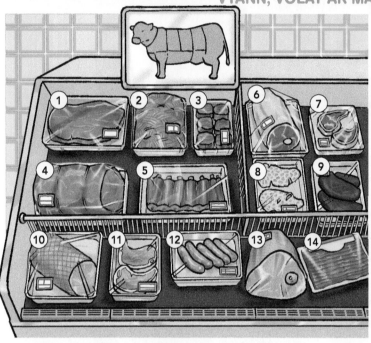

Vyann	**Meat**		kalè	**25**	flounder
biftèk	**1** steak		twit	**26**	trout
vyann moulen	**2** ground beef		pwason	**27**	catfish
vyann pou bouyon	**3** stewing beef		file pwason bale	**28**	filet of sole
wozbif/vyann bèf woti	**4** roast beef				
kòt	**5** ribs		PWASON NAN KOKI	SHELLFISH	
janm mouton	**6** leg of lamb		chèvrèt	**29**	shrimp
kotlèt mouton	**7** lamb chops		koki senjak	**30**	scallops
vant bèf/kochon	**8** tripe		krab	**31**	crabs
fwa	**9** liver		paloud	**32**	clams
kochon	**10** pork		moul	**33**	mussels
kotlèt kochon	**11** pork chops		zwit	**34**	oysters
sosis	**12** sausages		wonma	**35**	lobster
janbon	**13** ham				
bekonn	**14** bacon				

Volay	**Poultry**
poul	**15** chicken
blan poul	**16** chicken breasts
pye poul/	**17** chicken legs/
kwis poul	drumsticks
zèl poul	**18** chicken wings
kwis poul	**19** chicken thighs
kodenn	**20** turkey
kanna	**21** duck

Manje Lanmè	**Seafood**
PWASON	FISH
somon	**22** salmon
fletan	**23** halibut
pwason èglefen	**24** haddock

A. I'm going to the supermarket. What do we need?
B. Please get some **steak**.
A. **Steak**? All right.

A. Excuse me. Where can I find _____?
B. Look in the _____ Section.
A. Thank you.

A. This/These _____ looks/ look very fresh!
B. Let's get some for dinner.

Do you eat meat, poultry, or seafood?
Which of these foods do you like?

Which of these foods are popular in your coun

PWODUI LÈT, JI AK BWASON

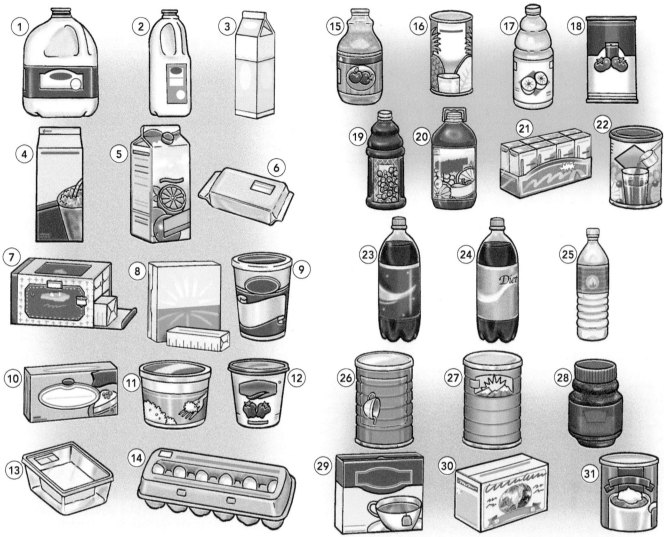

Pwodui lèt		Dairy Products
lèt	**1**	milk
lèt degrese	**2**	low-fat milk
ti lèt	**3**	skim milk
chokola ak lèt	**4**	chocolate milk
ji zoranj*	**5**	orange juice*
fwomaj	**6**	cheese
bè	**7**	butter
magarin/bè	**8**	margarine
lèt si	**9**	sour cream
krèm fwomaj	**10**	cream cheese
lèt kaye	**11**	cottage cheese
yogout	**12**	yogurt

tofou*	**13**	tofu*
ze	**14**	eggs

Ji		**Juices**
ji pòm	**15**	apple juice
ji zannanna	**16**	pineapple juice
ji chadèk	**17**	grapefruit juice
ji tomat	**18**	tomato juice
ji rezen	**19**	grape juice
ponch fwi	**20**	fruit punch
ti pake ji	**21**	juice paks
ji an poud	**22**	powdered drink mix

Bwason		Beverages
soda	**23**	soda
soda dyèt	**24**	diet soda
boutèy dlo	**25**	bottled water

Kafe ak te		Coffee and Tea
kafe	**26**	coffee
kafe dekafeyine/ kafe san kafeyin	**27**	decaffeinated coffee/decaf
kafe enstantane	**28**	instant coffee
te	**29**	tea
te fèy	**30**	herbal tea
chokola/chokola an poud	**31**	cocoa/hot chocolate mix

*Ji zoranj ak tofou pa gen lèt nan yo, men generalman, se nan seksyon sa w ap twouve yo.

A. I'm going to the supermarket to get some **milk**.
Do we need anything else?
B. Yes. Please get some **apple juice**.

A. Excuse me. Where can I find _____?
B. Look in the _____ Section.
A. Thanks.

A. Look! _____ is/are on sale this week!
B. Let's get some!

Which of these foods do you like?

Which of these foods are good for you?

Which brands of these foods do you buy?

CHAKITRI, MANJE GLASE AK FRIDÒDÒY

Chakitri	Deli		mozarèl	11	mozzarella	ji sitwon konjile/	21	frozen
wòzbif/vyann bèf woti	1	roast beef	fwonmaj cheda	12	cheddar cheese	glase/lemonad		lemonade
mòtadèl	2	bologna	salad ponmtè	13	potato salad	ji zoranj konjile/	22	frozen
salami	3	salami	kòlslo	14	cole slaw	glase		orange juice
janbon	4	ham	salad makawonni	15	macaroni salad			
kodenn	5	turkey	salad pasta	16	pasta salad	Fridòdòy		Snack Foods
kònbif	6	corned beef	salad manje lanmè	17	seafood salad	pòmdetè fri	23	potato chips
pastrami	7	pastrami				tòtiya fri	24	tortilla chips
fwonmaj swis	8	Swiss cheese	Manje glase		Frozen Foods	pretzel	25	pretzels
fwonmaj pwovolonn	9	provolone	krèmalaglas/krèm	18	ice cream	nwa	26	nuts
fwonmaj ameriken	10	American cheese	legim konjile/glase	19	frozen vegetables	pòpkon	27	popcorn
			dine konjile/glase	20	frozen dinners			

A. Should we get some **roast beef**?
B. Good idea. And let's get some **potato salad**.

[1–17]
A. May I help you?
B. Yes, please. I'd like some _____.

[1–27]
A. Excuse me. Where is/are _____?
B. It's/They're in the _____ Section.

What kinds of snack foods are popular in your country?

Are frozen foods common in your country? What kinds of foods are in the Frozen Foods Section?

EPISRI

Pwovizyon Alimantè	Packaged Goods
sereyal	**1** cereal
bonbon	**2** cookies
biswit soda	**3** crackers
makawonni	**4** macaroni
makawonni plat	**5** noodles
espageti	**6** spaghetti
diri	**7** rice

Manje nan fèblan	Canned Goods
soup	**8** soup
touna	**9** tuna (fish)
legim nan	**10** (canned)
fèblan	vegetables
fwi nan fèblan	**11** (canned) fruit

Konfiti ak Jele	Jams and Jellies
konfiti	**12** jam
jele	**13** jelly
manba	**14** peanut butter

Asezonnay	Condiments
sòs tonmat	**15** ketchup
moutad	**16** mustard
relich	**17** relish
pikliz	**18** pickles
oliv	**19** olives
sèl	**20** salt
pwav	**21** pepper
epis	**22** spices
sòs soya	**23** soy sauce
mayonnèz	**24** mayonnaise
luil/lwil (pou fè manje)	**25** (cooking) oil
luil/lwil oliv	**26** olive oil

salsa	**27** salsa
vinèg	**28** vinegar
sòs salad	**29** salad dressing

Manje nan fou	Baked Goods
pen	**30** bread
ti pen/pen won	**31** rolls
mèfin Angle	**32** English muffins
pen pita	**33** pita bread
gato	**34** cake

Founiti pou Gato	Baking Products
farin	**35** flour
sik	**36** sugar
gato an poud	**37** cake mix

A. I got **cereal** and **soup**. What else is on the shopping list?
B. **Ketchup** and **bread**.

A. Excuse me. I'm looking for _____.
B. It's/They're next to the _____.

A. Pardon me. I'm looking for _____.
B. It's/They're between the _____ and the _____.

Which of these foods do you like?

Which brands of these foods do you buy?

PWODUI POU KAY, PWODUI BEBE AK MANJE BÈT KAY

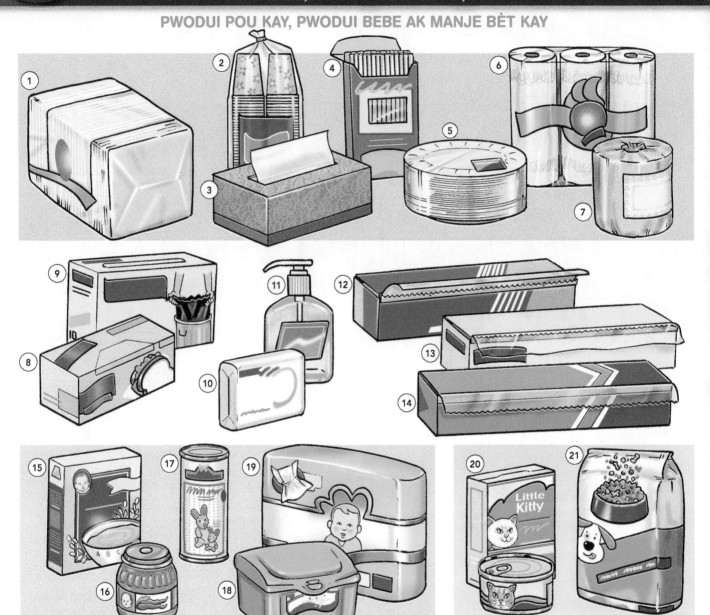

Pwodui an papye	Paper Products		Pwodui pou kay	Household Items		Pwodui Bebe	Baby Products
sèvyèt papye	**1** napkins		sache sandwich	**8** sandwich bags		sereyal bebe	**15** baby cereal
gode papye	**2** paper cups		sak pou fatra	**9** trash bags		manje bebe	**16** baby food
mouchwa papye	**3** tissues		savon	**10** soap		lèt bebe	**17** formula
chalimo	**4** straws		savon likid	**11** liquid soap		netwayèt bebe	**18** wipes
asyèt papye/katon	**5** paper plates		papye aliminyòm	**12** aluminum foil		kouchèt papye	**19** (disposable) diapers
tòchon papye	**6** paper towels		papye plastik pou vlope	**13** plastic wrap		**Manje Bèt Kay**	**Pet Food**
ijyenik	**7** toilet paper		papye sire	**14** waxed paper		manje chat	**20** cat food
						manje chyen	**21** dog food

A. Excuse me. Where can I find **napkins**?
B. **Napkins**? Look in Aisle 4.

[7, 10–17, 20, 21]
A. We forgot to get _____!
B. I'll get it. Where is it?
A. It's in Aisle _____.

[1–6, 8, 9, 18, 19]
A. We forgot to get _____!
B. I'll get them. Where are they?
A. They're in Aisle _____.

What do you need from the supermarket?
Make a complete shopping list!

SIPÈMAKÈT LA

ale/zèl	**1**	aisle
kliyan	**2**	shopper/customer
panyen makèt	**3**	shopping basket
liy kès	**4**	checkout line
kontwa kès	**5**	checkout counter
tapi woulan	**6**	conveyor belt
kès otomatik	**7**	cash register
charyo	**8**	shopping cart
chiklèt	**9**	(chewing) gum
sirèt	**10**	candy
koupon	**11**	coupons
kesye	**12**	cashier
sache papye	**13**	paper bag

anbalè	**14**	bagger/packer
liy	**15**	express checkout
esprès		(line)
jounal	**16**	tabloid (newspaper)
magazin	**17**	magazine
eskanè	**18**	scanner
sache plastik	**19**	plastic bag
pwodui	**20**	produce
dirijè/manadjè	**21**	manager
kesye	**22**	clerk
balans	**23**	scale
machin pou remèt fèblan	**24**	can-return machine
machin pou remèt boutèy	**25**	bottle-return machine

[1–8, 11–19, 21–25]
A. This is a gigantic supermarket!
B. It is! Look at all the **aisle**s!

[9, 10, 20]
A. This is a gigantic supermarket!
B. It is. Look at all the **produce**!

Where do you usually shop for food? Do you go to a supermarket, or do you go to a small grocery store? Describe the place where you shop.

Describe the differences between U.S. supermarkets and food stores in your country.

RESIPYAN AK KANTITE

sak/sache	**1**	bag	tèt	**9**	head
boutèy	**2**	bottle	bokal	**10**	jar
bwat	**3**	box	pen tranche	**11**	loaf–loaves
pat/pake/grap	**4**	bunch	pake	**12**	pack
bwat fèblan	**5**	can	anbalaj	**13**	package
katon	**6**	carton	woulo	**14**	roll
bwat	**7**	container	pake sis/sikspak	**15**	six-pack
douzèn*	**8**	dozen*			

baton	**16**	stick
tib	**17**	tube
pent	**18**	pint
ka	**19**	quart
demi-galon	**20**	half-gallon
galon	**21**	gallon
lit	**22**	liter
liv	**23**	pound

* "a dozen eggs," NOT "a dozen of eggs"

A. Please get a **bag** of *flour* when you go to the supermarket.
B. A **bag** of *flour*? Okay.

A. Please get two **bottles** of *ketchup* when you go to the supermarket.
B. Two **bottles** of *ketchup*? Okay.

[At home]

A. What did you get at the supermarket?
B. I got _____, _____, and _____.

[In a supermarket]

A. Is this the express checkout line?
B. Yes, it is. Do you have more than eight items?
A. No. I only have _____, _____, and _____.

Open your kitchen cabinets and refrigerator. Make a list of all the things you find.

What do you do with empty bottles, jars, and cans? Do you recycle them, reuse them, or throw them away?

PWA AK MEZI

kiyè kafe | teaspoon
tsp.

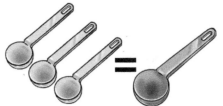

kiyè tab | tablespoon
Tbsp.

yon ons likid | 1 (fluid) ounce
1 fl. oz.

tas | cup
c.
8 ons likid | 8 fl. ozs.

pent | pint
pt.
16 ons likid | 16 fl. ozs.

ka | quart
qt.
32 ons likid | 32 fl. ozs.

galon | gallon
gal.
128 ons likid | 128 fl. ozs.

A. How much water should I put in?
B. The recipe says to add one _____ of water.

A. This fruit punch is delicious! What's in it?
B. Two _____s of apple juice, three _____ of orange juice, and a _____ of grape juice.

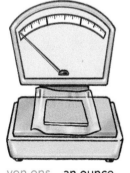

yon ons | an ounce

1 ons. | oz.

yon ka liiv | a quarter of a pound
1/4 liv | 1/4 lb.
4 ons. | 4 ozs.

demi liv | half a pound
1/2 liv | 1/2 lb.
8 ons. | 8 ozs.

twaka liv | three-quarters of a pound
3/4 liv | 3/4 lb.
12 ons. | 12 ozs.

yon liv | a pound
1 liv | lb.
16 ons. | 16 ozs.

A. How much roast beef would you like?
B. I'd like _____, please.
A. Anything else?
B. Yes. Please give me _____ of Swiss cheese.

A. This chili tastes very good! What did you put in it?
B. _____ of ground beef, _____ of beans, _____ of tomatoes, and _____ of chili powder.

PREPARASYON AK RESÈT POU KWIT MANJE

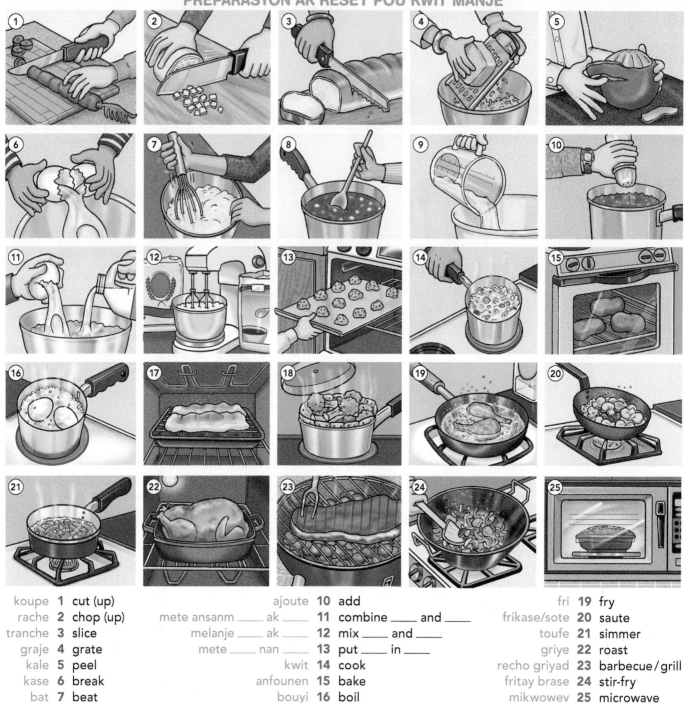

koupe	1	cut (up)
rache	2	chop (up)
tranche	3	slice
graje	4	grate
kale	5	peel
kase	6	break
bat	7	beat
brase	8	stir
vide	9	pour

ajoute	10	add
mete ansanm ____ ak ____	11	combine ____ and ____
melanje ____ ak ____	12	mix ____ and ____
mete ____ nan ____	13	put ____ in ____
kwit	14	cook
anfounen	15	bake
bouyi	16	boil
griye	17	broil
kwit nan vapè	18	steam

fri	19	fry
frikase/sote	20	saute
toufe	21	simmer
griye	22	roast
recho griyad	23	barbecue / grill
fritay brase	24	stir-fry
mikwowev	25	microwave

A. Can I help you?
B. Yes. Please **cut up** the vegetables.

[1–25]
A. What are you doing?
B. I'm _____ing the ....

[14–25]
A. How long should I _____ the ....?
B. _____ the .... for .... minutes/seconds.

What's your favorite recipe? Give instructions and use the units of measure on page 57. For example:

Mix a cup of flour and two tablespoons of sugar.
Add half a pound of butter.
Bake at 350° (degrees) for twenty minutes.

BATRI KWIZIN

louch pou krèm	**1**	ice cream scoop
ouvbwat	**2**	can opener
ouvboutèy	**3**	bottle opener
kouto legim	**4**	(vegetable) peeler
batèz	**5**	(egg) beater
kouvèti	**6**	lid/cover/top
bonm	**7**	pot
pwelon	**8**	frying pan/skillet
kaswòl vapè	**9**	double boiler
chodyè chinwa	**10**	wok
louch	**11**	ladle
paswa	**12**	strainer
espatil	**13**	spatula

chodyè pou kwit ak vapè	**14**	steamer
kouto	**15**	knife
krazè lay	**16**	garlic press
graj	**17**	grater
pirèks	**18**	casserole dish
plat pou fou	**19**	roasting pan
etajè pou fou	**20**	roasting rack
kouto file	**21**	carving knife
kaswòl	**22**	saucepan
paswa	**23**	colander
revèy pou kwizin	**24**	kitchen timer
woulo pat	**25**	rolling pin

plato tat	**26**	pie plate
kouto file	**27**	paring knife
plato bonbon	**28**	cookie sheet
moul pou dekoupe pat	**29**	cookie cutter
bòl melanj	**30**	(mixing) bowl
batèzamen	**31**	whisk
tas mezi	**32**	measuring cup
kiyè mezi	**33**	measuring spoon
plato gato	**34**	cake pan
kiyè bwa	**35**	wooden spoon

A. Could I possibly borrow your **ice cream scoop**?
B. Sure. I'll be happy to lend you my **ice cream scoop**.
A. Thanks.

A. What are you looking for?
B. I can't find the _____.
A. Look in that drawer/in that cabinet/ on the counter/next to the _____/ ....

[A Commercial]
Come to *Kitchen World*! We have everything you need for your kitchen, from _____s and _____s, to _____s and _____s. Are you looking for a new _____? Is it time to throw out your old _____? Come to *Kitchen World* today! We have everything you need!

What kitchen utensils and cookware do you have in your kitchen?

Which things do you use very often?

Which things do you rarely use?

MANJE PRESE

anmbègè	**1**	hamburger	yogout konjile/glase	**15**	frozen yogurt
chizbègè	**2**	cheeseburger	lèt ak krèm/melkchek	**16**	milkshake
òtdòg	**3**	hot dog	soda	**17**	soda
sandwich pwason	**4**	fish sandwich	kouvèti	**18**	lids
sandwich poul	**5**	chicken sandwich	gode papye	**19**	paper cups
poul fri	**6**	fried chicken	chalimo	**20**	straws
ponmtè fri	**7**	french fries	sèvyèt papye	**21**	napkins
nachos	**8**	nachos	fouchèt ak kouto plastik	**22**	plastic utensils
tako	**9**	taco	sòs tonmat	**23**	ketchup
bourito	**10**	burrito	moutad	**24**	mustard
tranch pitza	**11**	slice of pizza	mayonnèz	**25**	mayonnaise
bòl chili	**12**	bowl of chili	relich	**26**	relish
salad	**13**	salad	sòs salad	**27**	salad dressing
krèm	**14**	ice cream			

A. May I help you?
B. Yes. I'd like a/an ___[1–5, 9–17]___ /
   an order of ___[6–8]___ .

A. Excuse me. We're almost out of
   ___[18–27]___ .
B. I'll get some more from the
   supply room. Thanks for telling
   me.

Do you go to fast-food restaurants? Which ones?
How often? What do you order?

Are there fast-food restaurants in your country?
Are they popular? What foods do they have?

MAGAZEN POU MANJE LEJE AK SANDWICH

dounòt	**1** donut	chokola cho	**20** hot chocolate
ponmkèt	**2** muffin	lèt	**21** milk
begèl	**3** bagel	sandwich pwason touna	**22** tuna fish sandwich
pen lèt	**4** bun	sandwich salad ze	**23** egg salad sandwich
patistri	**5** danish/pastry	sandwich salad poul	**24** chicken salad sandwich
biswit	**6** biscuit	sandwich janbon	**25** ham and cheese
kwasan	**7** croissant	ak fomaj	sandwich
ze	**8** eggs	sandwich kònbif	**26** corned beef sandwich
pannkek	**9** pancakes	BLT/sandwich bekonn,	**27** BLT/bacon, lettuce,
wafal	**10** waffles	leti ak tonmat	and tomato sandwich
pen griye	**11** toast	sandwich wozbif	**28** roast beef sandwich
la	**12** bacon	pen blan	**29** white bread
sosis	**13** sausages	pen ble	**30** whole wheat bread
pòmtè fri	**14** home fries	pen pita	**31** pita bread
kafe	**15** coffee	pen nwa	**32** pumpernickel
kafe dekafeyine	**16** decaf coffee	pen sèg	**33** rye bread
te	**17** tea	pen won	**34** a roll
te glase	**18** iced tea	pen long	**35** a submarine roll
limonnad	**19** lemonade		

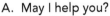

A. May I help you?
B. Yes. I'd like a _____[1–7]_____/an order of _____[8–14]_____, please.
A. Anything to drink?
B. Yes. I'll have a small/medium-size/large/extra-large
_____[15–21]_____.

A. I'd like a _____[22–28]_____ on _____[29–35]_____, please.
B. What do you want on it?
A. Lettuce/tomato/mayonnaise/mustard/. . .

Do you like these foods? Which ones? Where do you get them? How often do you have them?

RESTORAN AN

mete kliyan yo chita	**A**	seat the customers	chèz pou wose bebe	**7** booster seat
vide dlo a	**B**	pour the water	meni	**8** menu
pran kòmann lan	**C**	take the order	panyen pen	**9** bread basket
sèvi manje a	**D**	serve the meal	moun ki ranmase asyèt	**10** busperson
			madmwazèl/sèvant	**11** waitress/server
otès	**1**	hostess	gason/sèvant	**12** waiter/server
obèjis	**2**	host	bifè salad	**13** salad bar
kliyan	**3**	diner/patron/customer	kote pou manje	**14** dining room
konpatiman	**4**	booth	kwizin	**15** kitchen
tab	**5**	table	kizinye	**16** chef
chèz wo pou bebe	**6**	high chair		

[4–9]

A. Would you like a **booth**?
B. Yes, please.

[10–12]

A. Hello. My name is *Julie*, and I'll be your **waitress** this evening.
B. Hello.

[1, 2, 13–16]

A. This restaurant has a wonderful **salad bar**.
B. I agree.

netwaye tab la	**E**	clear the table	bòl soup	**26**	soup bowl
peye chèk la	**F**	pay the check	vè pou dlo	**27**	water glass
kite tep	**G**	leave a tip	vè pou diven	**28**	wine glass
ranje tab la	**H**	set the table	tas	**29**	cup
			soukoup	**30**	saucer
chanm pou asyèt	**17**	dishroom	sèvyèt papye	**31**	napkin
machin vesèl	**18**	dishwasher			
plato	**19**	tray	**ajantri**		**silverware**
charèt desè	**20**	dessert cart	fouchèt salad	**32**	salad fork
bòdwo	**21**	check	fouchèt pou manje aswè	**33**	dinner fork
tep/poubwa/kichòy	**22**	tip	kouto	**34**	knife
plat salad	**23**	salad plate	ti kiyè	**35**	teaspoon
plat pen ak bè	**24**	bread-and-butter plate	kiyè soup	**36**	soup spoon
asyèt manje aswè	**25**	dinner plate	kouto bè	**37**	butter knife

[A–H]
A. Please _____.
B. All right. I'll _____ right away.

[23–37]
A. Excuse me. Where does the _____ go?
B. It goes ⎰ to the left of the _____.
             to the right of the _____.
             on the _____.
             between the _____ and the _____.

[1, 2, 10–12, 16, 18]
A. Do you have any job openings?
B. Yes. We're looking for a _____.

[23–37]
A. Excuse me. I dropped my _____.
B. That's okay. I'll get you another _____ from the kitchen.

Tell about a restaurant you know. Describe the place and the people. (Is the restaurant large or small? How many tables are there? How many people work there? Is there a salad bar? . . .)

MENI RESTORAN AN

tas fwi	1	fruit cup/ fruit cocktail	vyann moulen	12	meatloaf	gato chokola	24	chocolate cake
ji tomat	2	tomato juice	vyann bèf	13	roast beef/prime rib	tat pòm	25	apple pie
koktèl kribich	3	shrimp cocktail	poul nan fou	14	baked chicken	krèmalaglas	26	ice cream
zèl poul	4	chicken wings	pwason bouyi	15	broiled fish	jelo	27	jello
nachos	5	nachos	vèmisèl ak boulèt	16	spaghetti and meatballs	poudin	28	pudding
po ponmtè	6	potato skins				sonnde	29	ice cream sundae
			kòtlèt vo	17	veal cutlet			
salad vèt	7	tossed salad/ garden salad	pòmtè lan fou	18	a baked potato			
salad grèk	8	Greek salad	pire ponmtè	19	mashed potatoes			
salad zepina	9	spinach salad	pòmtè fri	20	french fries			
antipasto	10	antipasto (plate)	diri	21	rice			
salad Seza	11	Caesar salad	vèmisèl	22	noodles			
			legim melanje	23	mixed vegetables			

[Ordering dinner]
A. May I take your order?
B. Yes, please. For the appetizer, I'd like the _____ [1–6] .
A. And what kind of salad would you like?
B. I'll have the _____ [7–11] .
A. And for the main course?
B. I'd like the _____ [12–17] , please.
A. What side dish would you like with that?
B. Hmm. I think I'll have _____ [18–23] .

[Ordering dessert]
A. Would you care for some dessert?
B. Yes. I'll have _____ [24–28] /an _____ [29] .

Tell about the food at a restaurant you know. What's on the menu?

What are some typical foods on the menus of restaurants in your country?

KOULÈ

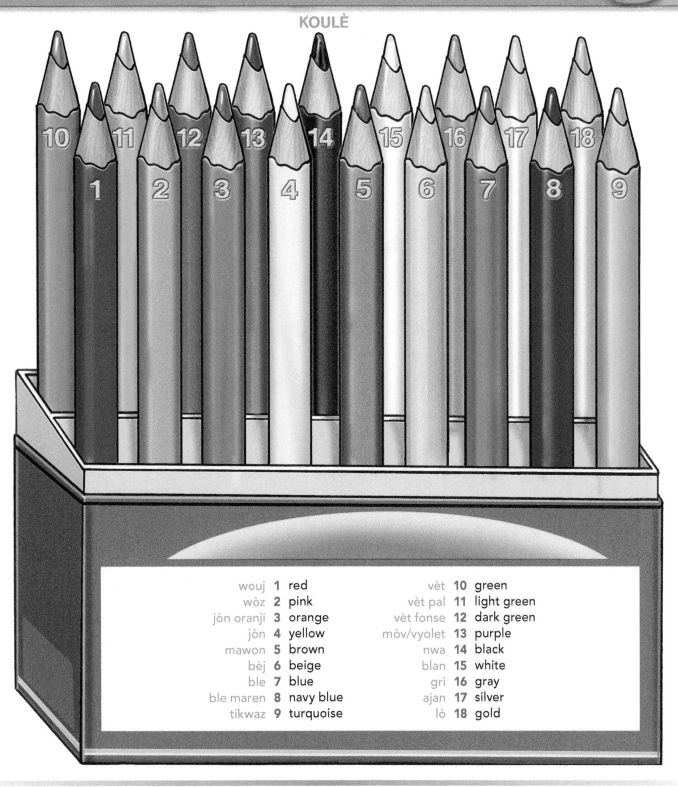

wouj	**1**	red		
wòz	**2**	pink		
jòn oranji	**3**	orange		
jòn	**4**	yellow		
mawon	**5**	brown		
bèj	**6**	beige		
ble	**7**	blue		
ble maren	**8**	navy blue		
tikwaz	**9**	turquoise		
vèt	**10**	green		
vèt pal	**11**	light green		
vèt fonse	**12**	dark green		
mòv/vyolet	**13**	purple		
nwa	**14**	black		
blan	**15**	white		
gri	**16**	gray		
ajan	**17**	silver		
lò	**18**	gold		

A. What's your favorite color?
B. **Red**.

A. I like your _____ shirt.
   You look very good in _____.

B. Thank you. _____ is my
   favorite color.

A. My TV is broken.
B. What's the matter with it?
A. People's faces are _____,
   the sky is _____, and the
   grass is _____!

Do you know the flags of different countries?
What are the colors of flags you know?

What color makes you happy? What color
makes you sad? Why?

RAD

kòsaj	**1**	blouse	manto espò/	**11**	sport coat/
jip	**2**	skirt	vès espò		sport jacket/jacket
chemiz	**3**	shirt	kostim	**12**	suit
pantalon	**4**	pants/slacks	kostim twa pyès	**13**	three-piece suit
chemiz espò	**5**	sport shirt	kravat	**14**	tie/necktie
djin	**6**	jeans	inifòm	**15**	uniform
mayo	**7**	knit shirt/jersey	chemizèt ak	**16**	T-shirt
wòb	**8**	dress	manch		
chanday	**9**	sweater	pantalon kout	**17**	shorts
levit	**10**	jacket	rad gwosès	**18**	maternity dress
			rad yon pyès	**19**	jumpsuit

jile	**20**	vest
rad toudinpyès	**21**	jumper
vès kwaze	**22**	blazer
rad/tounik/kazak	**23**	tunic
kolan	**24**	leggings
salopèt	**25**	overalls
chanday kòl wo	**26**	turtleneck
esmokin	**27**	tuxedo
wozèt	**28**	bow tie
wòb long	**29**	(evening) gown

A. I think I'll wear my new **blouse** today.
B. Good idea!

A. I really like your _____.
B. Thank you.
A. Where did you get it/them?
B. At ....

A. Oh, no! I just ripped
my _____!
B. What a shame!

What clothing items in this lesson do you wear?

What color clothing do you like to wear?

What do you wear at work or at school? at parties?
at weddings?

RAD POU FREDI

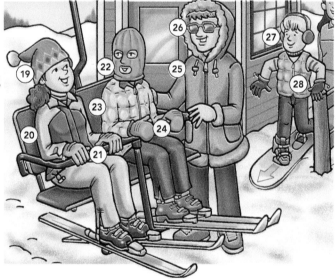

manto	**1** coat	parabriz	**11** windbreaker	gan	**21** gloves
manto	**2** overcoat	padsi	**12** raincoat	mask eski	**22** ski mask
chapo	**3** hat	chapo pou lapli	**13** rain hat	jakèt kapitonnen	**23** down jacket
blouzon	**4** jacket	padsi kwaze	**14** trench coat	gan sandwèt	**24** mittens
echap	**5** scarf/muffler	parapli	**15** umbrella	manto eskimo	**25** parka
vès chanday	**6** sweater jacket	poncho	**16** poncho	linèt solèy	**26** sunglasses
kolan	**7** tights	jakèt lapli	**17** rain jacket	pwotèj zorèy	**27** ear muffs
kaskèt	**8** cap	bòt lapli	**18** rain boots	jile kapitonnen	**28** down vest
vès kui	**9** leather jacket	chapo eski	**19** ski hat		
kaskèt bisbòl	**10** baseball cap	jakèt eski	**20** ski jacket		

A. What's the weather like today?
B. It's cool/cold/raining/snowing.
A. I think I'll wear my _____.

[1–6, 8–17, 19, 20, 22, 23, 25, 28]
A. May I help you?
B. Yes, please. I'm looking for a/an _____.

[7, 18, 21, 24, 26, 27]
A. May I help you?
B. Yes, please. I'm looking for _____.

What do you wear outside when the weather is cool?/when it's raining?/when it's very cold?

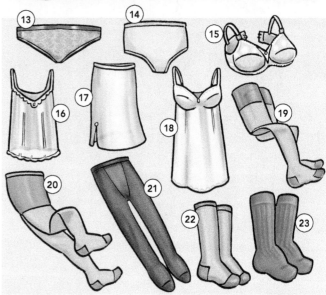

pijama	**1** pajamas	jòki/slip **8** (jockey) shorts/ underpants/briefs
chemizdennwit	**2** nightgown	kalson **9** boxer shorts/boxers
long		sipò atletik/ **10** athletic supporter/
chemizdennwit	**3** nightshirt	sispanswa jockstrap
kout		kalson long **11** long underwear/
wòbdechanm	**4** bathrobe/robe	long johns
pantouf	**5** slippers	chosèt **12** socks
kostim triko/	**6** blanket sleeper	kilòt **13** (bikini) panties
kostim lenn		slip/ **14** briefs/
chemizèt	**7** undershirt/T-shirt	kilòt underpants

soutyen	**15** bra
kamizòl	**16** camisole
bout jipon	**17** half slip
jipon	**18** (full) slip
ba	**19** stockings
ba kilòt	**20** pantyhose
kolan	**21** tights
chosèt long	**22** knee-highs
ba/chosèt long	**23** knee socks

A. I can't find my new _____.
B. Did you look in the bureau/dresser/closet?
A. Yes, I did.
B. Then it's/they're probably in the wash.

What sleepwear items do you wear? What sleepwear items do people in your family wear?

RAD POU EGZÈSIS AK SOULYE

chemizèt san manch	**1** tank top	rad kouvri kostimdeben	**9** cover-up	soulye tenis	**18** tennis shoes
chòt espò/ chòt pou kouri	**2** running shorts	kostimdeben	**10** swimsuit/ bathing suit	soulye kous	**19** running shoes
bando espò	**3** sweatband			bòt tenis	**20** high-tops/ high-top sneakers
kostim espò	**4** jogging suit/ running suit/ warm-up suit	chòt	**11** swimming trunks/ swimsuit/ bathing suit	sandal	**21** sandals
chemizèt ak manch	**5** T-shirt	leyota	**12** leotard	sapat	**22** thongs/ flip-flops
kolan espò	**6** lycra shorts/ bike shorts	soulye	**13** shoes	bòt	**23** boots
		talon kikit	**14** (high) heels	bòt pou travay	**24** work boots
chemizèt espò	**7** sweatshirt	soulye fèmen	**15** pumps	bòt montay	**25** hiking boots
pantalon espò	**8** sweatpants	soulye mokasen	**16** loafers	bòt kòbòy	**26** cowboy boots
		tennis	**17** sneakers/ athletic shoes	mokasen	**27** moccasins

[1–12]
A. Excuse me. I found this/these _____ in the dryer. Is it/Are they yours?
B. Yes. It's/They're mine. Thank you.

[13–27]
A. Are those new _____?
B. Yes, they are.
A. They're very nice.
B. Thanks.

Do you exercise? What do you do?
What kind of clothing do you wear when you exercise?

What kind of shoes do you wear when you go to work or to school? when you exercise? when you relax at home?
when you go out with friends or family members?

bag	**1**	ring	medalyon	**10**	locket	pòtfèy
bag fiyansay	**2**	engagement ring	brasle	**11**	bracelet	sentiwon
alyans	**3**	wedding ring/ wedding band	barèt	**12**	barrette	bous/sakamanch

bag **1** ring
bag fiyansay **2** engagement ring
alyans **3** wedding ring/ wedding band
zanno **4** earrings
kolye **5** necklace
kolye pèl **6** pearl necklace/ pearls/ string of pearls
chenn **7** chain
krizokal **8** beads
bròch **9** pin/brooch

medalyon **10** locket
brasle **11** bracelet
barèt **12** barrette
bouton manch **13** cuff links
bretèl **14** suspenders
mont **15** watch/ wrist watch
mouchwa **16** handkerchief
pòt kle **17** key ring/ key chain
ti bous **18** change purse

pòtfèy **19** wallet
sentiwon **20** belt
bous/sakamanch **21** purse/ handbag/ pocketbook
valiz **22** shoulder bag
sakamen **23** tote bag
sakaliv/valiz liv **24** book bag
sakado/bakpak **25** backpack
valiz makiyaj **26** makeup bag
valiz/sakí **27** briefcase

A. Oh, no! I think I lost my **ring**!
B. I'll help you look for it.

A. Oh, no! I think I lost my **earrings**!
B. I'll help you look for them.

[In a store]
A. Excuse me. Is this/Are these _____ on sale this week?
B. Yes. It's/They're half price.

[On the street]
A. Help! Police! Stop that man/woman!
B. What happened?!
A. He/She just stole my _____ and my _____!

Do you like to wear jewelry? What jewelry do you have?

In your country, what do men, women, and children use to carry their things?

DESKRIPSYON RAD

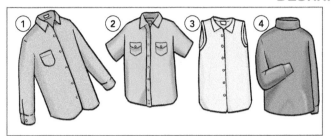
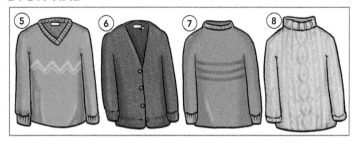
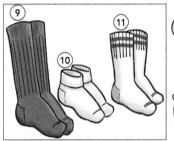

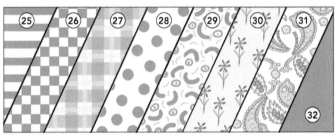
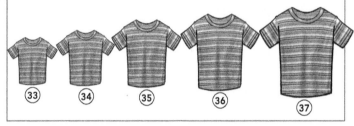

Kalite Rad		Types of Clothing
chemiz manch long	1	long-sleeved shirt
chemiz manch kout	2	short-sleeved shirt
chemiz san manch	3	sleeveless shirt
Kòl wo/Kòl woule	4	turtleneck (shirt)
chanday kou an V	5	V-neck sweater
chanday lenn	6	cardigan sweater
chanday kou maren	7	crewneck sweater
chanday kòl monte	8	turtleneck sweater
ba long	9	knee-high socks
chosèt je pye	10	ankle socks
chosèt long	11	crew socks
zanno pèse	12	pierced earrings
zanno plake	13	clip-on earrings

Kalite Materyèl		Types of Material
pantalon vlou kotle	14	corduroy *pants*
bòt kui	15	leather *boots*
ba naylon	16	nylon *stockings*
mayo koton	17	cotton *T-shirt*
blouzon kaki ble	18	denim *jacket*
chemiz flannèl	19	flannel *shirt*
kòsaj polièstè	20	polyester *blouse*
rad lenn	21	linen *dress*
echap swa	22	silk *scarf*
chanday lenn	23	wool *sweater*
chapo pay	24	straw *hat*

Desen		Patterns
ak ba	25	striped
ak kawo	26	checked
twal ekosè	27	plaid
rad ak boul	28	polka-dotted
enprime	29	patterned/print
twal ak flè	30	flowered/floral
kachmi	31	paisley
ble ini	32	solid *blue*

Mezi		Sizes
tou piti	33	extra-small
piti	34	small
medyòm/ mwayèn	35	medium
laj/gwo	36	large
laj anpil	37	extra-large

[1–24]
A. May I help you?
B. Yes, please. I'm looking for a *shirt*.*
A. What kind?
B. I'm looking for a *long-sleeved shirt*.

* With 9–16: I'm looking for _____.

[25–32]
A. How do you like this _____ tie/shirt/skirt?
B. Actually, I prefer that _____ one.

[33–37]
A. What size are you looking for?
B. _____.

Describe your favorite clothing items. For each item, tell about the color, the type of material, the size, and the pattern.

PWOBLÈM RAD AK CHANJMAN

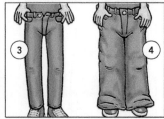
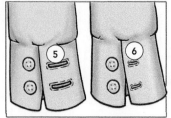
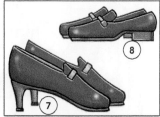

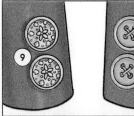

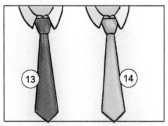
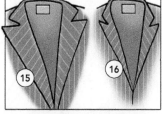

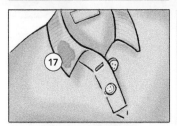
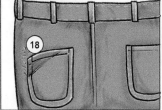

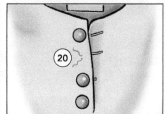

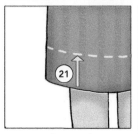
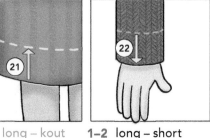

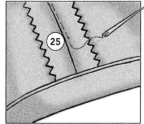

long – kout	**1–2** long – short	*kòlèt* tache	**17** stained *collar*
sere – bagi	**3–4** tight – loose/baggy	*pòch* chire	**18** ripped/torn *pocket*
laj/gwo – piti	**5–6** large/big – small	*zip* kase	**19** broken *zipper*
wo – ba	**7–8** high – low	*bouton* manke	**20** missing *button*
bòzò – senp	**9–10** fancy – plain	monte *jip la*	**21** shorten the *skirt*
lou – leje	**11–12** heavy – light	lonje *manch yo*	**22** lengthen the *sleeves*
fonse – klè	**13–14** dark – light	fèmen *jile a*	**23** take in the *jacket*
laj – etwat	**15–16** wide – narrow	laji *pantalon an*	**24** let out the *pants*
		ranje/repare *kouti a*	**25** fix/repair the *seam*

[1–2]
A. Are the sleeves too **long**?
B. No. They're too **short**.

1–2   Are the sleeves too _____?
3–4   Are the pants too _____?
5–6   Are the buttonholes too _____?
7–8   Are the heels too _____?

9–10   Are the buttons too _____?
11–12   Is the coat too _____?
13–14   Is the color too _____?
15–16   Are the lapels too _____?

[17–20]
A. What's the matter with it?
B. It has a **stained** collar.

[21–25]
A. Please **shorten** the *skirt*.
B. **Shorten** the *skirt*? Okay.

Tell about the differences between clothing people wear now and clothing people wore a long time ago.

LESIV

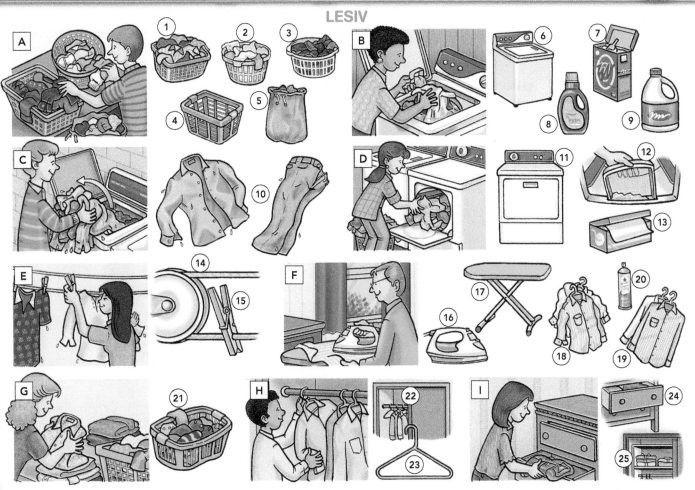

separe lesiv la	**A**	sort the laundry
mete lesiv la nan machin nan	**B**	load the washer
retire rad yo nan machin nan	**C**	unload the washer
mete rad yo nan chechwa a	**D**	load the dryer
kwoke rad yo sou liyn nan	**E**	hang clothes on the clothesline
fè pou pase	**F**	iron
pliye/kase rad yo	**G**	fold the laundry
kwoke rad yo	**H**	hang up clothing
mete bagay yo an plans	**I**	put things away

lesiv	**1**	laundry
rad klè	**2**	light clothing
rad koulè fonse	**3**	dark clothing
panyen lesiv	**4**	laundry basket
sak lesiv	**5**	laundry bag
machinalave	**6**	washer/washing machine
savon lesiv	**7**	laundry detergent
ramoli pou rad	**8**	fabric softener
kloròks	**9**	bleach

rad mouye	**10**	wet clothing
machin pou cheche	**11**	dryer
aparèy pou ranmase kras	**12**	lint trap
dekolan	**13**	static cling remover
rad		
liy lesiv	**14**	clothesline
pens rad	**15**	clothespin
fè pou pase	**16**	iron
tap pou pase	**17**	ironing board
rad chifonnen	**18**	wrinkled clothing
rad pase	**19**	ironed clothing
mete lanmidon	**20**	spray starch
rad pwop	**21**	clean clothing
klozèt	**22**	closet
sèso	**23**	hanger
tiwa	**24**	drawer
etaj	**25**	shelf-shelves

[A–I]
A. What are you doing?
B. I'm _____ing.

[4–6, 11, 14–17, 23]
A. Excuse me. Do you sell _____s?
B. Yes. They're at the back of the store.
A. Thank you.

[7–9, 13, 20]
A. Excuse me. Do you sell _____?
B. Yes. It's at the back of the store.
A. Thank you.

Who does the laundry in your home? What things does this person use?

MAGAZEN VARYETE

tablo enfòmasyon	**1**	(store) directory
kontwa Bijou	**2**	Jewelry Counter
kontwa Pafen	**3**	Perfume Counter
eskalye woulant	**4**	escalator
asansè	**5**	elevator
Depatman rad gason	**6**	Men's Clothing Department
zòn livrezon machandiz	**7**	customer pickup area
Depatman rad fanm	**8**	Women's Clothing Department
Depatman rad timoun	**9**	Children's Clothing Department

Depatman bagay kay	**10**	Housewares Department
Depatman mèb	**11**	Furniture Department/ Home Furnishings Department
Depatman aparèy menaje	**12**	Household Appliances Department
Depatman elektwonik	**13**	Electronics Department
kontwa Sèvis Kliyan	**14**	Customer Assistance Counter/ Customer Service Counter
chanm gason	**15**	men's room
chanm fi	**16**	ladies' room
fontèn dlo	**17**	water fountain
magazen ti goute	**18**	snack bar
kontwa Papye Kado	**19**	Gift Wrap Counter

A. Excuse me. Where's the **store directory**?
B. It's over there, next to the **Jewelry Counter**.
A. Thanks.
B. You're welcome.

A. Excuse me. Do you sell *ties**?
B. Yes. You can find *ties** in the ____[6, 8–13]____ /at the ____[2, 3]____ on the first/second/third/fourth floor.
A. Thank you.

*ties/bracelets/dresses/toasters/. . .

Describe a department store you know. Tell what is on each floor.

AP ACHTE

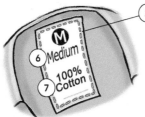

achte	**A**	buy
remèt	**B**	return
chanje	**C**	exchange
eseye/mezire	**D**	try on
peye	**E**	pay for
pran enfòmasyon	**F**	get some information about

siy vant	**1**	sale sign
etikèt	**2**	label
etikèt pri	**3**	price tag
resi	**4**	receipt
rabè	**5**	discount
mezi	**6**	size
materyèl	**7**	material

enstriksyon pou okipe rad	**8**	care instructions
pri nòmal	**9**	regular price
pri pou vant	**10**	sale price
pri	**11**	price
taks sou lavant	**12**	sales tax
pri total	**13**	total price

A. May I help you?
B. Yes, please. I want to _____[A–F]_____ this item.
A. Certainly. I'll be glad to help you.

A. { What's the _____[5–7, 9–13]_____ ?
   { What are the _____[8]_____ ?
B. _____ .
A. Are you sure?
B. Yes. Look at the _____[1–4]_____ !

Which stores in your area have sales? How often?

Tell about something you bought on sale.

VIDEYO AK EKIPMAN ODYO

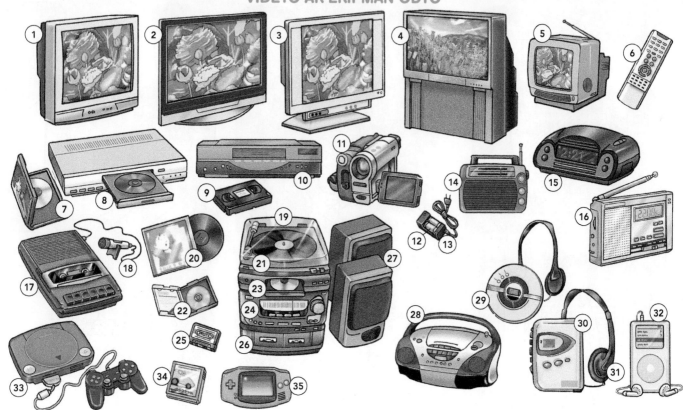

televizyon	**1** TV/television	sistèm estereyo	**19** stereo system/ sound system
televizyon plazma	**2** plasma TV	plak	**20** record
televizyon LCD	**3** LCD TV	toundis	**21** turntable
televizyon pwojeksyon	**4** projection TV	CD	**22** CD/compact disc
televizyon pòtatif	**5** portable TV	aparèy CD	**23** CD player
kontwòl adistans	**6** remote (control)	sentonizè	**24** tuner
DVD	**7** DVD	odyo tep/kasèt	**25** (audio)tape/(audio)cassette
aparèy DVD	**8** DVD player	kasètofòn	**26** tape deck/cassette deck
videyo/kasèt videyo/ vidyotep	**9** video/videocassette/ videotape	wopalè	**27** speakers
VCR	**10** VCR/videocassette recorder	aparèy estereyo pòtab/ pèsonnèl	**28** portable stereo system/ boombox
Kodak/kamera/ videyo	**11** camcorder/ video camera	aparèy CD pòtab/ pèsonnèl	**29** portable/personal CD player
pake pil	**12** battery pack	aparèy kasèt pòtatif	**30** portable/personal cassette player
aparèy chaje batri	**13** battery charger	ekoutè	**31** headphones
radyo	**14** radio	aparèy pòtab dijital pou tande	**32** portable/personal digital audio player
radyo revèy	**15** clock radio	sistèm jwèt videyo	**33** video game system
radyo onn kout	**16** shortwave radio	jwèt videyo	**34** video game
anrejistrè tep	**17** tape recorder/ cassette recorder	jwèt videyo pòtab	**35** hand-held video game
mikwo	**18** microphone		

A. May I help you?
B. Yes, please. I'm looking for a **TV**.

With 27 & 31, use: I'm looking for _____.

A. I like your new _____. Where did you get it/them?

B. At .....(name of store).....

A. Which company makes the best _____?

B. In my opinion, the best _____ is/are made by ....

What video and audio equipment do you have or want?

In your opinion, which brands of video and audio equipment are the best?

telefòn	**1**	telephone/phone	regilatè voltaj	**12**	voltage regulator
telefòn san kòd	**2**	cordless phone	adaptè	**13**	adapter
telefòn selilè	**3**	cell phone/cellular phone	kamera (35milimèt)	**14**	(35 millimeter) camera
batri/pil	**4**	battery	vè	**15**	lens
aparèy pou chaje batri/pil	**5**	battery charger	film	**16**	film
			vè zoum	**17**	zoom lens
repondè	**6**	answering machine	kamera dijital	**18**	digital camera
pejè	**7**	pager	disk memwa	**19**	memory disk
PDA/òganayzè pèsonnèl	**8**	PDA/electronic personal organizer	trepye	**20**	tripod
			flach (atachman)	**21**	flash (attachment)
aparèy faks	**9**	fax machine	valiz pou kamera	**22**	camera case
(pòch) kalkilatè	**10**	(pocket) calculator	pwojektè eslay	**23**	slide projector
machinakalkile	**11**	adding machine	ekran (sinema)	**24**	(movie) screen

A. Can I help you?
B. Yes. I want to buy a **telephone**.*

* With 16, use: I want to buy _____.

A. Excuse me. Do you sell
    _____s?*

B. Yes. We have a large
    selection of _____s.

* With 16, use the singular.

A. Which _____ is the best?

B. This one here. It's made by
    .....(company)......

What kind of telephone do you use?

Do you have a camera? What kind is it?
What do you take pictures of?

Does anyone you know have an answering machine?
When you call, what message do you hear?

KONPITÈ

Materyèl Enfòmatik		Computer Hardware
konpitè	1	(desktop) computer
CPU	2	CPU/central processing unit
monitè/ekran	3	monitor/screen
CD-ROM drive	4	CD-ROM drive
CD-ROM	5	CD-ROM
disk pwosesè	6	disk drive
diskèt	7	(floppy) disk
klavye	8	keyboard
sourit	9	mouse

monitè plat/ ekran LCD	10	flat panel screen/ LCD screen
konpitè pòtab	11	notebook computer
bwa pou dirije	12	joystick
boul pou dirije	13	track ball
modèm	14	modem
pwoteksyon kont gwo voltaj	15	surge protector
enprimant	16	printer
eskanè/eskritè	17	scanner
kab	18	cable

Lojisyèl konpitè		Computer Software
pwogram mo	19	word-processing program
pwogram kontablite	20	spreadsheet program
pwogram lojisyèl edikasyon	21	educational software program
jwèt konpitè	22	computer game

A. Can you recommend a good **computer**?
B. Yes. This **computer** here is excellent.

A. Is that a new _____?
B. Yes.
A. Where did you get it?
B. At ......(name of store).........

A. May I help you?
B. Yes, please. Do you sell _____s?
A. Yes. We carry a complete line of _____s.

Do you use a computer? When?

In your opinion, how have computers changed the world?

jwèt pou tab	**1**	board game	ti machin jwèt	**14**	matchbox car	liv pou kolorye	**27** coloring book
jwèt pasyans	**2**	(jigsaw) puzzle	kamyon jwèt	**15**	toy truck	papye bristòl	**28** construction paper
jwèt konstriksyon	**3**	construction set	jwèt machin kous	**16**	racing car set		
jwèt blòk	**4**	(building) blocks	jwèt tren	**17**	train set	bwat penti	**29** paint set
boul kawotchou	**5**	rubber ball	model jwèt	**18**	model kit	patamodle	**30** (modeling) clay
balon plaj	**6**	beach ball	pou sanble			etikèt kolan	**31** stickers
bokit ak pèl	**7**	pail and shovel	jwèt syans	**19**	science kit	bisiklèt	**32** bicycle
pope	**8**	doll	wòkitòki	**20**	walkie-talkie (set)	trisik	**33** tricycle
rad pope	**9**	doll clothing	woulawoup	**21**	hula hoop	kabwèt	**34** wagon
kay pope	**10**	doll house	kòd pou sote	**22**	jump rope	planch ak woulèt/	**35** skateboard
mèb pope	**11**	doll house furniture	boul kim savon	**23**	bubble soap	esketbòd	
			koleksyon kat	**24**	trading cards	balanswa	**36** swing set
pèsonnaj jwèt	**12**	action figure	kreyon koulè	**25**	crayons	kay jwèt	**37** play house
bèt boure	**13**	stuffed animal	makè	**26**	(color) markers	pisin plastik	**38** kiddie pool/ inflatable pool

A. Excuse me. I'm looking for (a/an) _____(s) for my *grandson*.*
B. Look in the next aisle.
A. Thank you.

* *grandson/granddaughter/. . .*

A. I don't know what to get my ....-year-old son/daughter for his/her birthday.
B. What about (a) _____?
A. Good idea! Thanks.

A. Mom/Dad? Can we buy this/these _____?
B. No, *Johnny*. Not today.

What toys are most popular in your country?

What were your favorite toys when you were a child?

BANK LAN

fè yon depo	**A**	make a deposit
fè yon tiraj	**B**	make a withdrawal
touché yon chèk	**C**	cash a check
achte chèk	**D**	get traveler's checks
ouvri yon kont	**E**	open an account
aplike pou prete lajan	**F**	apply for a loan
chanje lajan	**G**	exchange currency
fich depo	**1**	deposit slip
fich tiraj	**2**	withdrawal slip
chèk	**3**	check

chèk pou vwayaje	**4**	traveler's check
kanè labank	**5**	bankbook/passbook
kat ATM	**6**	ATM card
kat kredi	**7**	credit card
kavo	**8**	(bank) vault
bwat depo	**9**	safe deposit box
kesye	**10**	teller
ajan sekirite	**11**	security guard
machin tiraj otoèmatik/ machin ATM	**12**	ATM (machine)/ cash machine
ofisye labank	**13**	bank officer

[A–G]
A. Where are you going?
B. I'm going to the bank.
I have to _____.

[5–7]
A. What are you looking for?
B. My _____. I can't find it anywhere!

[8–13]
A. How many _____s does the State Street Bank have?
B. ....

Do you have a bank account? What kind? Where? What do you do at the bank?

Do you ever use traveler's checks? When?

Do you have a credit card? What kind? When do you use it?

FINANS

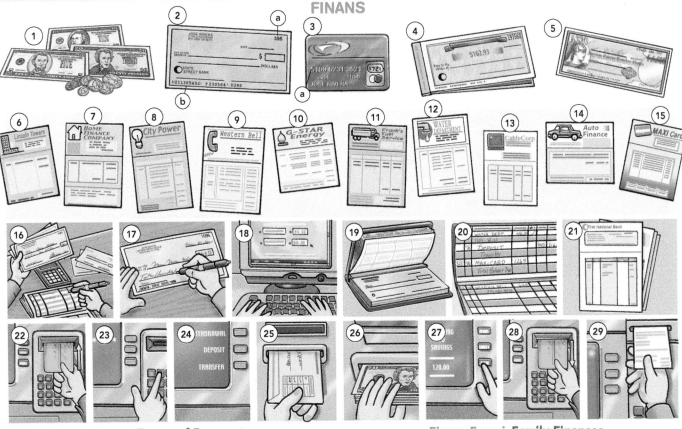

Jan pou Peye — Forms of Payment

lajan	**1**	cash
chèk	**2**	check
nimewo chèk	**a**	check number
nimewo kont	**b**	account number
kat kredi	**3**	credit card
nimewo kat kredi	**a**	credit card number
monnenòdè	**4**	money order
chèk vwayaj	**5**	traveler's check

Bòdwo Kay — Household Bills

lwaye	**6**	rent
pòtèk	**7**	mortgage payment
bil/bòdwo elektrik	**8**	electric bill
bil telefòn	**9**	telephone bill
bil/bòdwo gaz	**10**	gas bill
bil/bòdwo luil/chofaj	**11**	oil bill/heating bill
bil/bòdwo dlo	**12**	water bill
bil/bòdwo kab	**13**	cable TV bill
peye machin nan	**14**	car payment
bil/bòdwo kat kredi	**15**	credit card bill

Finans Fanmi — Family Finances

balanse kannè chek la	**16**	balance the checkbook
ekri yon chèk	**17**	write a check
bank nan konpitè	**18**	bank online
kannè chèk	**19**	checkbook
fèy kontwòl chèk	**20**	check register
eta kont pa mwa	**21**	monthly statement

Sèvi ak machin ATM — Using an ATM Machine

mete kat ATM nan andedan	**22**	insert the ATM card
mete nimewo PIN nan	**23**	enter your PIN number/personal identification number
chwazi yon tranzaksyon	**24**	select a transaction
fè yon depo	**25**	make a deposit
pran/retire lajan	**26**	withdraw/get cash
transfere fon/lajan	**27**	transfer funds
retire kat la	**28**	remove your card
pran resi a	**29**	take your transaction slip/receipt

A. Can I pay by ___[1, 2]___ / with a ___[3–5]___ ?
B. Yes. We accept ___[1]___ / ___[2–5]___ s.

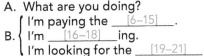

A. What are you doing?
B. { I'm paying the ___[6–15]___ .
{ I'm ___[16–18]___ ing.
{ I'm looking for the ___[19–21]___ .

A. What should I do?
B. ___[22–29]___ .

What household bills do you receive? How much do you pay for the different bills?

Who takes care of the finances in your household? What does that person do?

Do you use ATM machines? If you do, how do you use them?

LAPÒS LA

lèt	**1** letter	
kat postal	**2** postcard	
lèt	**3** air letter/	
avyon	aerogramme	
pake/koli	**4** package/parcel	
prenmyè klas	**5** first class	
lèt priyorite	**6** priority mail	
lèt	**7** express mail/	
esprès	overnight mail	
koli postal	**8** parcel post	
lèt sètifye	**9** certified mail	
tenm	**10** stamp	
fèy tenm	**11** sheet of stamps	

woulo tenm	**12** roll of stamps
kannè tenm	**13** book of stamps
monnyòdè	**14** money order
fòm pou	**15** change-of-
chanje adrès	address form
fòm pou anwole	**16** selective service
nan lame	registration form
fòm aplikasyon	**17** passport
pou paspò	application
	form
anvlòp	**18** envelope
adrès retounen	**19** return address
adrès	**20** mailing address

kòd postal	**21** zip code
so lapòs	**22** postmark
kantite tenm	**23** stamp/
	postage
fant pou lèt	**24** mail slot
anplwaye lapòs	**25** postal worker/
	postal clerk
balans	**26** scale
machin tenm	**27** stamp machine
faktè	**28** letter carrier/
	mail carrier
kamyon lapòs	**29** mail truck
bwat lèt	**30** mailbox

[1–4]
A. Where are you going?
B. To the post office. I have to mail a/an _____.

[5–9]
A. How do you want to send it?
B. _____, please.

[10–17]
A. Next!
B. I'd like a _____, please.
A. Here you are.

[19–21, 23]
A. Do you want me to mail this letter?
B. Yes, thanks.
A. Oops! You forgot the _____!

How often do you go to the post office? What do you do there?   Tell about the postal system in your country.

BIBLIYOTÈK LA

katalòg liv nan konpitè	**1**	online catalog	seksyon jounal ak magazin	**10**	periodical section	liv lang etranje	**22**	foreign language books
katalòg liv sou kat	**2**	card catalog	revi	**11**	journals	seksyon liv pou referans	**23**	reference section
òtè/moun ki ekri liv la	**3**	author	magazin	**12**	magazines	mikwofilm	**24**	microfilm
tit	**4**	title	jounal	**13**	newspapers	lekti sou mikwofilm	**25**	microfilm reader
kat bibliyotèk	**5**	library card	seksyon odyovizyèl	**14**	media section	diksyonnè	**26**	dictionary
machin fotokopi	**6**	copier/ photocopier/ copy machine	liv sou tep	**15**	books on tape	ansiklopedi	**27**	encyclopedia
			odyo tep yo/ kasèt yo	**16**	audiotapes	atlas	**28**	atlas
			CD	**17**	CDs	biwo referans	**29**	reference desk
etajè	**7**	shelves	videyo/tep	**18**	videotapes	bibliyotekè referans	**30**	(reference) librarian
seksyon pou timoun	**8**	children's section	(konpitè) lojisyèl	**19**	(computer) software	kontwa sikilasyon liv	**31**	checkout desk
liv pou timoun	**9**	children's books	DVD	**20**	DVDs	asistan bibliyotekè	**32**	library clerk
			seksyon lang etranje	**21**	foreign language section			

[1, 2, 6–32]

A. Excuse me. Where's/Where are the _____?

B. Over there, at/near/next to the _____.

[8–23, 26–28]

A. Excuse me. Where can I find a/an __[26–28]__ / __[9, 11–13, 15–20, 22]__ ?

B. Look in the __[8, 10, 14, 21, 23]__ over there.

A. I'm having trouble finding a book.

B. Do you know the __[3–4]__ ?

A. Yes. ....

A. Excuse me. I'd like to check out this __[26–28]__ /these __[11–13]__ .

B. I'm sorry. It/They must remain in the library.

Do you go to a library? Where? What does this library have?

Tell about how you use the library.

In the image:

COPIES

BOOK 1 of 10 Entries
TITLE: Cat's pajamas
AUTHOR: Bradbury, Ray
CALL NUMBER: 841.238
STATUS: Checked out

Public Library
Amy L. Jackson

BEAU

ENSTISYON KOMINOTE

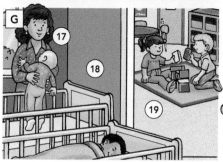

estasyon lapolis	A	police station
estasyon ponpye	B	fire station
lopital	C	hospital
meri	D	town hall/city hall
sant distraksyon	E	recreation center
baskil	F	dump
gadri	G	child-care center
sant pou granmoun	H	senior center
legliz	I	church
sinagòg	J	synagogue
moske	K	mosque
tanp	L	temple
èd nan ijans	1	emergency operator
ajan lapolis	2	police officer
machin polis	3	police car
machin ponpye	4	fire engine

ponpye	5	firefighter
sal dijans	6	emergency room
EMT/teknisyen ijans medikal	7	EMT/paramedic
anbilans	8	ambulance
majistra	9	mayor/city manager
chanm reyinyon	10	meeting room
jim	11	gym
direktè aktivite	12	activities director
chanm jwèt	13	game room
pisin	14	swimming pool
travayè vwari	15	sanitation worker
sant resiklaj	16	recycling center
anplwaye gadri	17	child-care worker
gadri	18	nursery
chanm pou jwe	19	playroom
anplwaye nan sant granmoun	20	eldercare worker/ senior care worker

[A–L]
A. Where are you going?
B. I'm going to the _____.

[1, 2, 5, 7, 12, 15, 17, 20]
A. What do you do?
B. I'm a/an _____.

[3, 4, 8]
A. Do you hear a siren?
B. Yes. There's a/an _____ coming up behind us.

What community institutions are in your city or town? Where are they located?

Which community institutions do you use? When?

KRIM AK IJANS

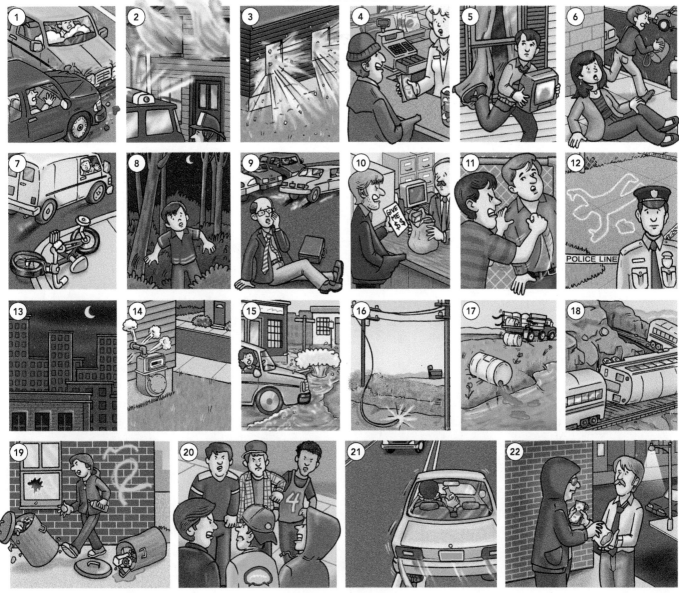

Haitian Creole	#	English
aksidan machin	1	car accident
dife	2	fire
eksplozyon	3	explosion
vòl	4	robbery
kase kay	5	burglary
vòle moun nan lari	6	mugging
kidnapin	7	kidnapping
timoun pèdi	8	lost child
vòl machin	9	car jacking
vòl bank	10	bank robbery
atake fizikman	11	assault
touye moun	12	murder
fè nwa	13	blackout/ power outage
gaz k ap koule	14	gas leak
gwo tiyo kase	15	water main break
liyn elektrisite kase	16	downed power line
gazpiyaj chimik	17	chemical spill
tren deraye	18	train derailment
detwi pwopriyete moun	19	vandalism
vyolans gang	20	gang violence
kondi machin tou sou	21	drunk driving
vann dwòg	22	drug dealing

[1–13]
A. I want to report a/an _____.
B. What's your location?
A. ....

[14–18]
A. Why is this street closed?
B. It's closed because of a _____.

[19–22]
A. I'm very concerned about the amount of _____ in our community.
B. I agree. _____ is a very serious problem.

Is there much crime in your community? Tell about it.

Have you ever experienced a crime or emergency? What happened?

THE BODY

KÒ MOUN

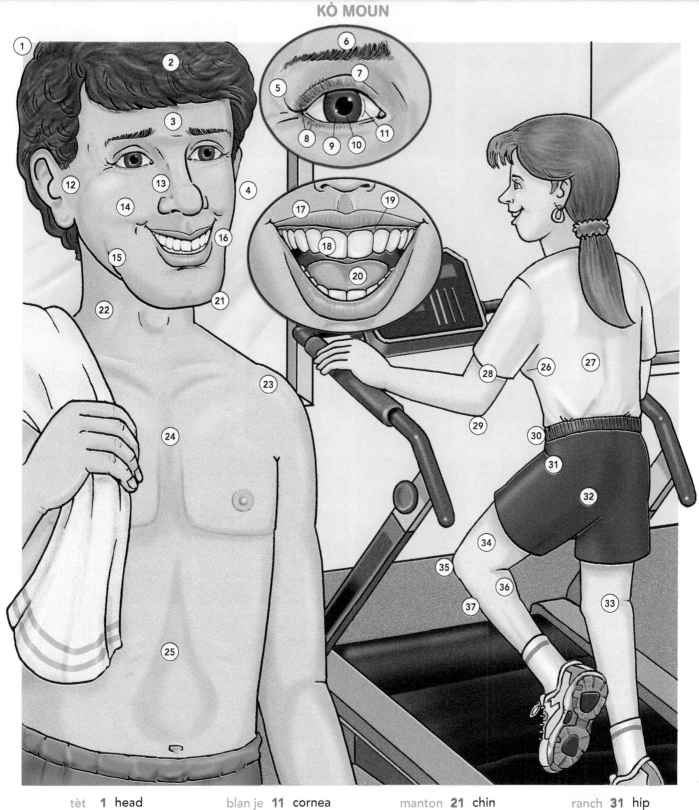

tèt	**1**	head	blan je	**11**	cornea	manton	**21**	chin	ranch	**31**	hip
cheve	**2**	hair	zorèy	**12**	ear	kou	**22**	neck	deyè	**32**	buttocks
fwon	**3**	forehead	nen	**13**	nose	zepòl	**23**	shoulder	janm	**33**	leg
figi	**4**	face	ponmèt	**14**	cheek	pwatrin	**24**	chest	kwis	**34**	thigh
je	**5**	eye	machwa	**15**	jaw	vant	**25**	abdomen	jennou	**35**	knee
sousi	**6**	eyebrow	bouch	**16**	mouth	sen/tete	**26**	breast	mòlèt	**36**	calf
pòpyè	**7**	eyelid	po bouch	**17**	lip	do	**27**	back	zo janm	**37**	shin
pwal je	**8**	eyelashes	dan–dan	**18**	tooth–teeth	bra	**28**	arm			
iris/mitan je	**9**	iris	jansiv	**19**	gums	koud	**29**	elbow			
nwa je	**10**	pupil	lang	**20**	tongue	tay	**30**	waist			

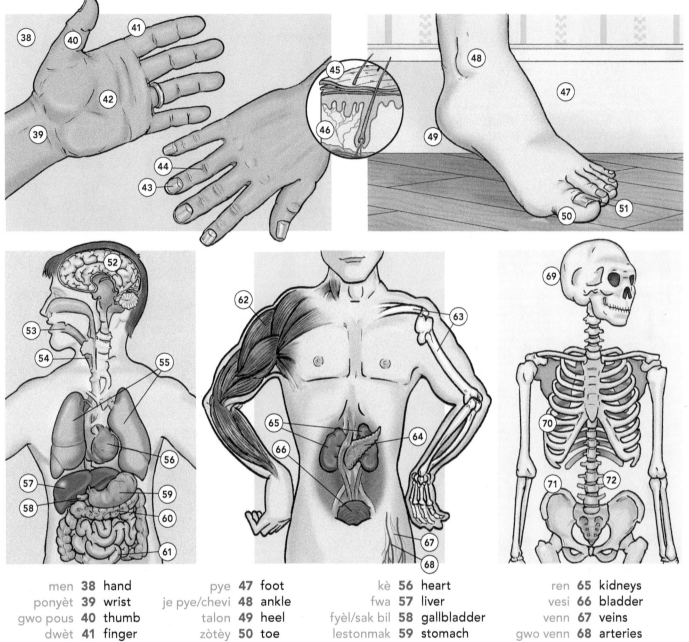

men	**38**	hand	pye	**47**	foot	kè	**56**	heart	
ponyèt	**39**	wrist	je pye/chevi	**48**	ankle	fwa	**57**	liver	
gwo pous	**40**	thumb	talon	**49**	heel	fyèl/sak bil	**58**	gallbladder	
dwèt	**41**	finger	zòtèy	**50**	toe	lestonmak	**59**	stomach	
pla men	**42**	palm	zong pye	**51**	toenail	gwo trip	**60**	large intestine	
zong dwèt	**43**	fingernail	sèvo	**52**	brain	ti trip	**61**	small intestine	
jwenti dwèt	**44**	knuckle	gòj	**53**	throat	mis	**62**	muscles	
po	**45**	skin	ezofaj	**54**	esophagus	zo	**63**	bones	
nè	**46**	nerve	poumon	**55**	lungs	pankreyas	**64**	pancreas	

ren	**65**	kidneys
vesi	**66**	bladder
venn	**67**	veins
gwo venn	**68**	arteries
zo tèt	**69**	skull
kòt	**70**	ribcage
anba vant	**71**	pelvis
jikibb rèldo/ mwèl rèldo	**72**	spinal column/ spinal cord

A. My doctor checked my **head** and said everything is okay.
B. I'm glad to hear that.

[1, 3–7, 12–29, 31–51]

A. Ooh!
B. What's the matter?
{ My _____ hurts!
{ My _____ s hurt!

[52–72]

A. My doctor wants me to have some tests.
B. Why?
A. She's concerned about my _____.

Describe yourself as completely as you can.

Which parts of the body are most important at school? at work? when you play your favorite sport?

MALADI, SENTÒM AK BLESI

  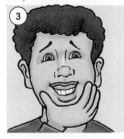 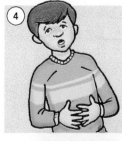 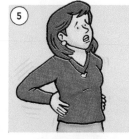

   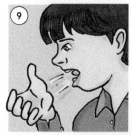 

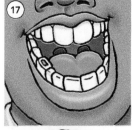 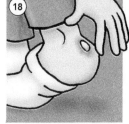 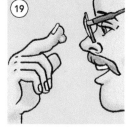  

maltèt	1	headache	enfeksyon	10	infection	siy	19	wart
malzòrèy	2	earache	gratèl	11	rash	wòkèt	20	(the) hiccups
maldan	3	toothache	piki moustik	12	insect bite	frison	21	(the) chills
doulè lestomak	4	stomachache	koutsolèy	13	sunburn	kranp	22	cramps
doulè do	5	backache	kou rèd	14	stiff neck	dyare	23	diarrhea
malgòj	6	sore throat	anrimen	15	runny nose	doulè pwatrin	24	chest pain
lafyèv/tanperati	7	fever/temperature	nen senyen	16	bloody nose	souf kout	25	shortness of breath
grip	8	cold	twou dan	17	cavity			
touse	9	cough	zanpoud	18	blister	larenjit	26	laryngitis

A. What's the matter?
B. I have a/an ___[1–19]___ .

A. What's the matter?
B. I have ___[20–26]___ .

endispoze	27 faint	touse	33 cough	pye tòdye	39 twist	ponyèt foule	46 sprain
vètij	28 dizzy	etènen	34 sneeze	grate	40 scratch		
bay lanoze/ fè dekonpoze	29 nauseous	esoufle	35 wheeze	kòche	41 scrape	disloke	47 dislocate
		wote	36 burp	mètri	42 bruise	kase–kase	48 break–broke
ayik	30 bloated	vomi	37 vomit/ throw up	boule	43 burn	anfle	49 swollen
konjesyonnen	31 congested			fè mal–fè mal	44 hurt–hurt	grate	50 itchy
bouke	32 exhausted	senyen	38 bleed	koupe–koupe	45 cut–cut		

A. What's the problem?
B. { I feel [27–30] .
I'm [31–32] .
I've been [33–38] ing a lot.

A. What happened?
B. { I [39–45] ed my ....
I think I [46–48] ed my ....
My .... is/are [49–50] .

A. How do you feel?
B. Not so good./Not very well./Terrible!
A. What's the matter?
B. ...., ..., and ....
A. I'm sorry to hear that.

Tell about the last time you didn't feel well. What was the matter?

Tell about a time you hurt yourself. What happened? How? What did you do about it?

What do you do when you have a cold? a stomachache? an insect bite? the hiccups?

PREMYE SEKOU

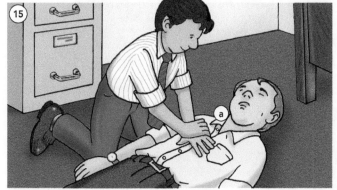

liv premye sekou	**1** first-aid manual	aspirin	**13** aspirin
bwat premye sekou	**2** first-aid kit	analjezik	**14** non-aspirin pain reliever
bandaj/pansman	**3** (adhesive) bandage/ Band-Aid™	reyannimasyon kadyo pilmonè	**15** CPR (cardiopulmonary resuscitation)
sèvyèt antiseptik pou netwaye	**4** antiseptic cleansing wipe	pa gen pou	**a** has no pulse
tanpon/gaz esterilize	**5** sterile (dressing) pad	respirasyon bouch nan bouch	**16** rescue breathing
dlo oksijene	**6** hydrogen peroxide	li pap respire	**b** isn't breathing
pomad antibyotik	**7** antibiotic ointment	manèv Heymlik	**17** the Heimlich maneuver
gaz	**8** gauze	ap toufe	**c** is choking
adeziv	**9** adhesive tape	èsplint/2 bwa pou kontrole fakti	**18** splint
pens	**10** tweezers	kase yon dwèt	**d** broke a finger
krèm antihistamin	**11** antihistamine cream	tournikèt	**19** tourniquet
bandaj/ pansman elastik	**12** elastic bandage/ Ace™ bandage	l ap senyen	**e** is bleeding

A. Do we have any ____[3–5, 12]___s/ ___[6–11, 13, 14]___?
B. Yes. Look in the first-aid kit.

A. Help! My friend ___[a–e]___!
B. I can help!
   { I know how to do ___[15–17]___.
   { I can make a ___[18, 19]___.

Do you have a first-aid kit? If you do, what's in it? If you don't, where can you buy one?

Tell about a time when you gave or received first aid.

Where can a person learn first aid in your community?

IJANS MEDIKAL AK MALADI

doulè	**1** hurt/injured	gòj enfekte	**14** strep throat
sezisman	**2** in shock	saranpyon	**15** measles
endispoze	**3** unconscious	malmouton	**16** mumps
kout chalè	**4** heatstroke	lawoujòl	**17** chicken pox
brili solèy	**5** frostbite	asm	**18** asthma
kriz kè	**6** heart attack	kansè	**19** cancer
reaksyon alèji	**7** allergic reaction	tristès/depresyon	**20** depression
vale pwazon	**8** swallow poison	dyabèt	**21** diabetes
pran yon dòz depase/ ovèdoz/medikaman	**9** overdose on drugs	maladi kè	**22** heart disease
tonbe/te tonbe	**10** fall–fell	tansyon	**23** high blood pressure/ hypertension
pran/te pran yon chòk elektrik	**11** get–got an electric shock	tebe/tibèkilez	**24** TB/tuberculosis
gripe/flou	**12** the flu/influenza	SIDA	**25** AIDS*
enfeksyon nan zòrèy	**13** an ear infection	* Sendwòm Iminize Defisitèman Aki	* Acquired Immune Deficiency Syndrome

A. What happened?

B. My ....
{
is _____ [1–3] .
has _____ [4–5] .
is having a/an _____ [6–7] .
_____ [8–11] ed.
}

A. What's your location?
B. .... (address) .

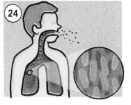 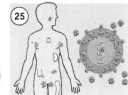

A. My .... is sick.
B. What's the matter?
A. He/She has _____ [12–25] .
B. I'm sorry to hear that.

Tell about a medical emergency that happened to you or someone you know.

Which illnesses in this lesson are you familiar with?

EGZAMEN MEDIKAL

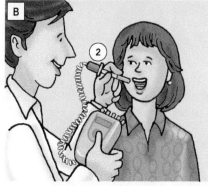
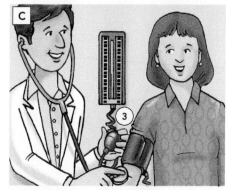
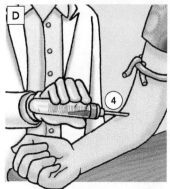
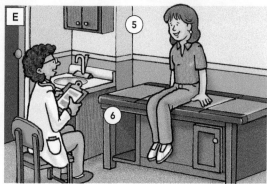

mezire otè ak pwa	**A**	measure *your* height and weight	balans	**1**	scale
pran tanperati	**B**	take *your* temperature	tèmonmèt	**2**	thermometer
tcheke tansyon ou	**C**	check *your* blood pressure	mezi tansyon	**3**	blood pressure gauge
pran san	**D**	draw some blood	egiy	**4**	needle/syringe
mande w kesyon sou sante ou	**E**	ask *you* some questions about *your* health	chanm konsilatsyon	**5**	examination room
ekzamine je, zorèy, nen, ak gòj ou	**F**	examine *your* eyes, ears, nose, and throat	tab konsiltasyon	**6**	examination table
koute batman kè ou	**G**	listen to *your* heart	kat pou li	**7**	eye chart
pran Eks-re(X-ray)/ radyografi pwatrin	**H**	take a chest X-ray	estetoskop	**8**	stethoscope
			machin X-ray/ machin radyografi	**9**	X-ray machine

[A–H]

A. Now I'm going to **measure your height and weight**.

B. All right.

[A–H]

A. What did the doctor/nurse do during the examination?

B. She/He **measured my height and weight**.

[1–3, 5–9]

A. So, how do you like our new **scale?**

B. It's very nice, doctor.

How often do you have a medical exam? What does the doctor/nurse do?

SWEN MEDIKAL AK SWEN DAN

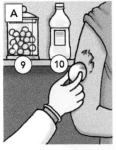
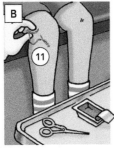

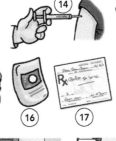
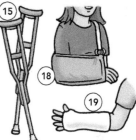
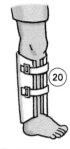

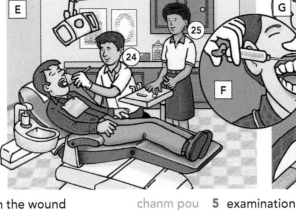
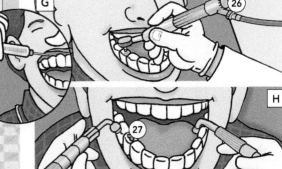

netwaye blese a	**A**	clean the wound
fèmen blese a	**B**	close the wound
panse blesi a	**C**	dress the wound
netwaye dan	**D**	clean *your* teeth
ekzamine dan ou	**E**	examine *your* teeth
bay yon piki anestezi	**F**	give *you* a shot of anesthetic/ Novocaine™
fouye twou dan an	**G**	drill the cavity
ranpli twou dan an	**H**	fill the tooth

chanm pou tann	**1**	waiting room
resepsyonis	**2**	receptionist
kat asirans	**3**	insurance card
fòm istwa medikal	**4**	medical history form

chanm pou konsilte	**5**	examination room
doktè	**6**	doctor/ physician
malad	**7**	patient
enfimyè	**8**	nurse
boul koton	**9**	cotton balls
alkòl	**10**	alcohol
kouti/koud yon blese	**11**	stitches
gaz	**12**	gauze
adeziv	**13**	tape
piki	**14**	injection/ shot

beki	**15**	crutches
pake glas	**16**	ice pack
preskripsyon	**17**	prescription
echap	**18**	sling
plat	**19**	cast
aparèy	**20**	brace
moun ki okipe ijèn	**21**	dental hygienist
mask	**22**	mask
gan	**23**	gloves
dantis	**24**	dentist
èd dantis	**25**	dental assistant
frèz	**26**	drill
plonbe/dan	**27**	filling

A. Now I'm going to
{ _____[A–H]_____.
give you (a/an) ___[14–17]___.
put your .... in a ___[18–20]___. }

B. Okay.

A. I need
{ ___[9, 10, 12, 13, 23]___.
a ___[22, 26]___. }

B. Here you are.

Tell about a personal experience you had with a medical or dental procedure.

KONSÈY MEDIKAL

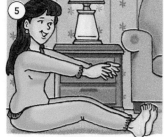

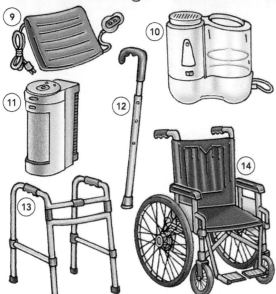

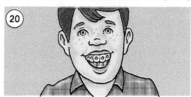

rete kouche	**1**	rest in bed	aparèy pou netwaye lè a	**11**	air purifier
bwè likid	**2**	drink fluids	baton	**12**	cane
gagari	**3**	gargle	aparèy pou mache	**13**	walker
fè dyèt	**4**	go on a diet	chèz woulant	**14**	wheelchair
ekzèsis	**5**	exercise	egzamen san	**15**	blood work/blood tests
pran vitamin	**6**	take vitamins	egzamen	**16**	tests
wè yon espesyalis	**7**	see a specialist	terapi pou kò	**17**	physical therapy
trètman ak egiy akiponkti	**8**	get acupuncture	operasyon	**18**	surgery
tanpon k ap bay chalè	**9**	heating pad	bay konsèy	**19**	counseling
aparèy imidite	**10**	humidifier	aparèy pou fikse dan	**20**	braces

A. I think
{ you should _____ [1–8].
you should use a/an _____ [9–14].
you need _____ [15–20]. }

B. I see.

A. What did the doctor say?

B. The doctor thinks
{ I should _____ [1–8].
I should use a/an _____ [9–14].
I need _____ [15–20]. }

Tell about medical advice a doctor gave you. What did the doctor say? Did you follow the advice?

MEDIKAMAN

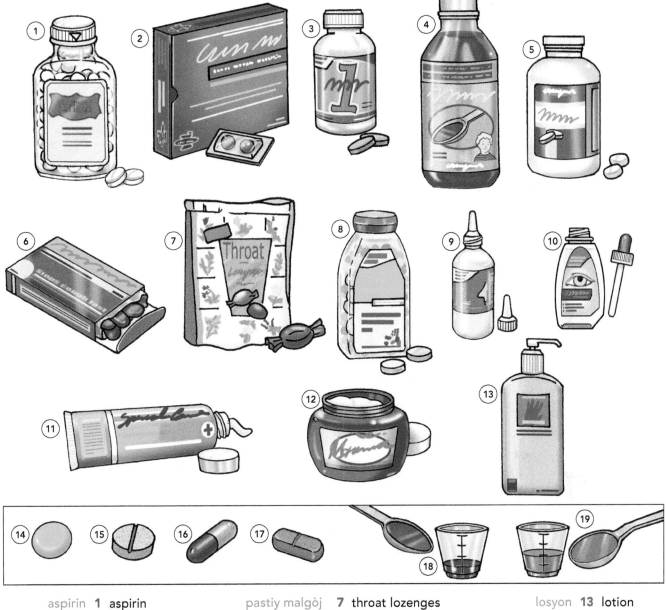

aspirin	**1**	aspirin
grenn pou grip	**2**	cold tablets
vitamin	**3**	vitamins
siwo tous	**4**	cough syrup
analjezik	**5**	non-aspirin pain reliever
gout pou tous	**6**	cough drops
pastiy malgòj	**7**	throat lozenges
pastiy kont asid	**8**	antacid tablets
vaporizatè nen	**9**	decongestant spray/ nasal spray
gout pou je	**10**	eye drops
ponmad	**11**	ointment
krèm	**12**	cream/creme
losyon	**13**	lotion
pilil/grenn	**14**	pill
pastiy	**15**	tablet
kapsil	**16**	capsule
tablet	**17**	caplet
kiyè kafe	**18**	teaspoon
kiyè tab	**19**	tablespoon

[1–13]

A. What did the doctor say?

B. { She/He told me to take ____[1–4]____ /a ____[5]____ .
{ She/He told me to use ____[6–13]____ .

[14–19]

A. What's the dosage?

B. One _____ every four hours.

What medicines in this lesson do you have at home? What other medicines do you have?

What do you take or use for a fever? a headache? a stomachache? a sore throat? a cold? a cough?

Tell about any medicines in your country that are different from the ones in this lesson.

ESPESYALIS MEDIKAL

  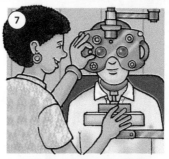 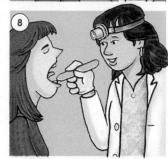

 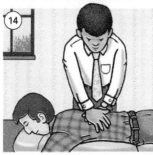 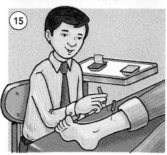 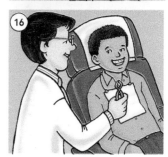

kadyològ/doktè kè	**1**	cardiologist
jinekològ	**2**	gynecologist
pedyat/doktè timoun	**3**	pediatrician
doktè pou granmoun	**4**	gerontologist
alejis	**5**	allergist
òtopedis	**6**	orthopedist
oftalmològ/doktè je	**7**	ophthalmologist
espesyalis zorèy, nen ak gòj	**8**	ear, nose, and throat (ENT) specialist

odyològ/doktè zòrèy	**9**	audiologist
fizyoterapis	**10**	physical therapist
terapis	**11**	counselor/therapist
sikyat	**12**	psychiatrist
gastwoantewolojis	**13**	gastroenterologist
kaywopraktè	**14**	chiropractor
teknisyen akiponkti	**15**	acupuncturist
òtodontis	**16**	orthodontist

A. I think you need to see a specialist.
   I'm going to refer you to a/an _____.
B. A/An _____?
A. Yes.

A. When is your next appointment with the _____?
B. It's at ....(time).... on ....(date)....

Do you or members of your family see any of these medical specialists? Which ones?

LOPITAL LA

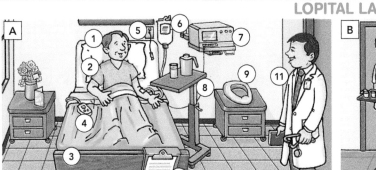

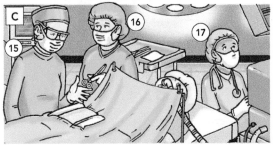

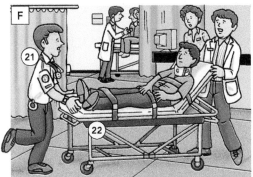
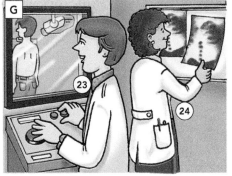

chanm pasyan	**A**	**patient's room**
pasyan	**1**	patient
chemiz lopital	**2**	hospital gown
kabann lopital	**3**	hospital bed
kontwòl kabann	**4**	bed control
sonnèt	**5**	call button
boutèy seròm	**6**	I.V.
aparèy kontwòl siy lavi	**7**	vital signs monitor
tab kabann	**8**	bed table
basen	**9**	bed pan
fèy sante	**10**	medical chart
doktè	**11**	doctor/physician

estasyon enfimyè	**B**	**nurse's station**
enfimyè	**12**	nurse
kontwolè rejim moun	**13**	dietitian
anplwaye lopital	**14**	orderly
sal operasyon	**C**	**operating room**
chirijyen	**15**	surgeon
enfimyè chirijyen	**16**	surgical nurse
anestezyolojis	**17**	anesthesiologist
chanm pou tann	**D**	**waiting room**
volontè	**18**	volunteer
sal akouchman	**E**	**birthing room / delivery room**
obstetrisyen	**19**	obstetrician
fanm saj	**20**	midwife/nurse-midwife

chanm ijan	**F**	**emergency room / ER**
teknisyen ijans medikal/EMT	**21**	emergency medical technician/EMT
kabann woulant	**22**	gurney
depatman radyoloji	**G**	**radiology department**
teknisyen radyografi	**23**	X-ray technician
radyolojis	**24**	radiologist
laboratwa	**H**	**laboratory/lab**
teknisyen laboratwa	**25**	lab technician

A. This is your ____[2–10]____.
B. I see.

A. Do you work here?
B. Yes. I'm a/an ____[11–21, 23–25]____.

A. Where's the ____[11–21, 23–25]____?
B. She's/He's { in the ____[A, C–H]____. at the ____[B]____.

Tell about an experience you or a family member had in the hospital.

IJÈN (PÈSONNÈL)

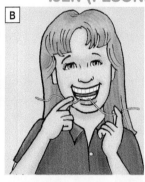

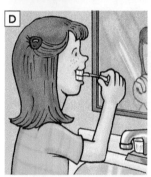

bwose dan *m*	**A**	**brush *my* teeth**
bwòsdan	**1**	toothbrush
pat	**2**	toothpaste
pase fil nan dan	**B**	**floss *my* teeth**
fil dantè	**3**	dental floss
gagari	**C**	**gargle**
lavay bouch	**4**	mouthwash
blanchi dan *m*	**D**	**whiten *my* teeth**
pat pou blanchi dan	**5**	teeth whitener
benyen	**E**	**bathe/take a bath**
savon	**6**	soap
kim pou benyen	**7**	bubble bath

pran yon douch	**F**	**take a shower**
chapo beny	**8**	shower cap
lave cheve *m*	**G**	**wash *my* hair**
chanpou	**9**	shampoo
kondisyonè	**10**	conditioner/rinse
seche cheve *m*	**H**	**dry *my* hair**
aparèy pou seche cheve	**11**	hair dryer/ blow dryer
penyen tèt mwen	**I**	**comb *my* hair**
peny	**12**	comb

bwose tèt mwen	**J**	**brush *my* hair**
bwòs tèt	**13**	(hair) brush
penyen tèt mwen alamòd	**K**	**style *my* hair**
fè	**14**	hot comb/ curling iron
vaporizatè cheve	**15**	hairspray
pat pou cheve	**16**	hair gel
zepeng cheve	**17**	bobby pin
barèt	**18**	barrette
pens pou cheve	**19**	hairclip

fè bab	**L**	**shave**		vèni pou zong	**31**	nail polish		losyon pou figi	**41**	moisturizer
krèm pou bab	**20**	shaving cream		asetòn	**32**	nail polish remover		poud	**42**	face powder
razwa	**21**	razor						makiyaj pou arebò zye	**43**	eyeliner
lam razwa	**22**	razor blade								
razwa elektrik	**23**	electric shaver		**mete . . .**	**N**	**put on . . .**		makiyaj popyè	**44**	eye shadow
kreyon estipik	**24**	styptic pencil		dezodoran	**33**	deodorant		maskara	**45**	mascara
losyon apre labab	**25**	aftershave (lotion)		losyon pou men	**34**	hand lotion		kreyon sousi	**46**	eyebrow pencil
				losyon pou kò	**35**	body lotion		woujalèv	**47**	lipstick
fè zong _mwen_	**M**	**do _my_ nails**		poud	**36**	powder				
lim zong an fè	**26**	nail file		pafen/ kolòy	**37**	cologne/ perfume		**netwaye soulye _mwen yo_**	**P**	**polish _my shoes_**
lim zong	**27**	emery board		krèm solèy	**38**	sunscreen		blakbòl/ekla	**48**	shoe polish
tay zong	**28**	nail clipper						lasèt	**49**	shoelaces
bwòs zong	**29**	nail brush		**makiye**	**O**	**put on makeup**				
sizo	**30**	scissors		fondten/fa jou	**39**	blush/rouge				
				krèm makiyaj	**40**	foundation/base				

[A–M, N (33–38), O, P]
A. What are you doing?
B. I'm _____ing.

[1, 8, 11–14, 17–19, 21–24, 26–30, 46, 49]
A. Excuse me. Where can I find _____(s)?
B. They're in the next aisle.

[2–7, 9, 10, 15, 16, 20, 25, 31–45, 47, 48]
A. Excuse me. Where can I find _____?
B. It's in the next aisle.

Which of these personal care products do you use?

You're going on a trip. Make a list of the personal care products you need to take with you.

SWEN BEBE

bay manje	**A**	**feed**
manje bebe	**1**	baby food
bavèt	**2**	bib
bibwon	**3**	bottle
tetin	**4**	nipple
lèt an poud	**5**	formula
vitamin an likid	**6**	(liquid) vitamins
chanje kouchèt	**B**	**change the**
bebe a		**baby's diaper**
kouchèt papye	**7**	disposable diaper
kouchèt twal	**8**	cloth diaper
zepeng kouchèt	**9**	diaper pin
papye ijenik	**10**	(baby) wipes
pou bebe		

poud pou bebe	**11**	baby powder
pantalon kouchèt pou	**12**	training pants
aprann al nan twalèt		
ponmad	**13**	ointment
benyen	**C**	**bathe**
chanpou bebe	**14**	baby shampoo
aplikatè	**15**	cotton swab
losyon bebe	**16**	baby lotion
kenbe	**D**	**hold**
sison	**17**	pacifier
jansivèt	**18**	teething ring
enfimyè	**E**	**nurse**

rad	**F**	**dress**
balanse	**G**	**rock**
gadri	**19**	child-care
		center
anplwaye	**20**	child-care
gadri		worker
chèz dodin	**21**	rocking chair
li	**H**	**read to**
kazye	**22**	cubby
jwe ak	**I**	**play with**
jwèt	**23**	toys

A. What are you doing?
B. { I'm _____[A, C–I]_____ing the baby.
     I'm _____[B]_____ing.

A. Do we need anything from the store?
B. Yes. We need some more { _____[2–4, 7–9, 15, 17, 18]_____ s
                                    _____[1, 5, 6, 10–14, 16]_____ .

In your opinion, which are better: cloth diapers or disposable diapers? Why?   Tell about baby products in your country.

DIFERAN KALITE LEKÒL

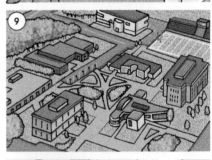

gadri	**1**	preschool/nursery school	kolèj kominote	**7**	community college
lekòl primè	**2**	elementary school	kolèj	**8**	college
lekòl segondè	**3**	middle school/ junior high school	invèsite	**9**	university
lekòl segondè/ klas imanitè	**4**	high school	lekòl metriz	**10**	graduate school
lekòl granmoun	**5**	adult school	lekòl dwa	**11**	law school
lekòl metye	**6**	vocational school/trade school	lekòl medikal	**12**	medical school

A. Are you a student?
B. Yes. I'm in _____[1–4, 8, 10–12]_____.

A. Are you a student?
B. Yes. I go to a/an _____[5–7, 9]_____.

A. Is this apartment building near a/an _____?
B. Yes. _____(name of school)_____ is nearby.

A. Tell me about your previous education.
B. I went to _____(name of school)_____.
A. Did you like it there?
B. Yes. It was an excellent _____.

What types of schools are there in your community? What are their names, and where are they located?

What types of schools have you gone to?

Where? When? What did you study?

LEKÒL LA

biwo	**A**	(main) office	teren kous	**I**	track	
biwo direktè	**B**	principal's office	estrad	**a**	bleachers	
enfimri/biwo enfimyè	**C**	nurse's office	teren espò	**J**	field	
biwo konseye	**D**	guidance office	oditoryòm	**K**	auditorium	
saldeklas	**E**	classroom	kafeterya	**L**	cafeteria	
koridò	**F**	hallway	bibliyotèk	**M**	library	
kazye elèv	**a**	locker				
laboratwa syans	**G**	science lab				
jimnazyòm	**H**	gym/gymnasium				
sal kazye elèv	**a**	locker room				

pwofesè	**5**	teacher
asistan direktè	**6**	assistant principal/ vice-principal
ofisye sekirite	**7**	security officer
pwofesè syans	**8**	science teacher
pwofesè edikasyon fizik	**9**	P.E. teacher
antrennè	**10**	coach
jeran	**11**	custodian
anplwaye kafeterya	**12**	cafeteria worker
siveyan kafeterya	**13**	lunchroom monitor
bibliyotèk lekòl	**14**	(school) librarian

sekretè lekòl	**1**	clerk/(school) secretary
direktè	**2**	principal
enfimyè	**3**	(school) nurse
konseyè	**4**	(guidance) counselor

A. Where are you going?
B. I'm going to the ___[A–D, G–M]___ .
A. Do you have a hall pass?
B. Yes. Here it is.

A. Where's the ___[1–14]___ ?
B. He's/She's in the ___[A–M]___ .

Describe the school where you study English. Tell about the rooms, offices, and people.

Tell about differences between the school in this lesson and schools in your country.

PWOGRAM LEKÒL

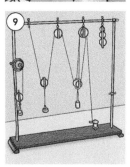

matematik	1	math/mathematics
angle	2	English
istwa	3	history
jewografi	4	geography
gouvènman	5	government
syans	6	science
byoloji	7	biology
chimi	8	chemistry
fizik	9	physics
sante	10	health
syans konpitè	11	computer science
espayòl	12	Spanish
franse	13	French
ekonomi domestik	14	home economics
atelye atizana	15	industrial arts/shop
edikasyon biznis	16	business education
edikasyon fizik	17	physical education/P.E.
leson kondi	18	driver's education/driver's ed
bèlte	19	art
mizik	20	music

A. What do you have next period?
B. **Math**. How about you?
A. **English**.
B. There's the bell. I've got to go.

What is/was your favorite subject? Why?

In your opinion, what's the most interesting subject? the most difficult subject? Why do you think so?

AKTIVITE APRE KLAS

òkès lekòl	**1**	band
òkès klasik	**2**	orchestra
koral	**3**	choir/chorus
teyat	**4**	drama
foutbòl Ameriken	**5**	football
ekip kap chofe	**6**	cheerleading/pep squad
etidyan gouvènman sipòte	**7**	student government
sèvis kominote	**8**	community service

jounal lekòl	**9**	school newspaper
liv souvni lekòl	**10**	yearbook
magazin literè	**11**	literary magazine
ekip odyo ak videyo	**12**	A.V. crew
klib deba	**13**	debate club
klib konpitè	**14**	computer club
klib entènasyonal	**15**	international club
klib echèk	**16**	chess club

A. Are you going home right after school?

B. { No. I have ___[1–6]___ practice.
{ No. I have a ___[7–16]___ meeting.

What extracurricular activities do/did you participate in?

Which extracurricular activities in this lesson are there in schools in your country? What other activities are there?

MATEMATIK

Arithmetic   Aritmetik

$$2+1=3 \qquad 8-3=5 \qquad 4\times2=8 \qquad 10\div2=5$$

adisyon **addition**	soustraksyon **subtraction**	miltiplikasyon **multiplication**	divizyon **division**
2 **plus** 1 **equals*** 3.	8 **minus** 3 **equals*** 5.	4 **times** 2 **equals*** 8.	10 **divided by** 2 **equals*** 5.

*You can also say: **is**

A. How much is *two plus one?*
B. *Two plus one* equals / is *three*.

Make conversations for the arithmetic problems above and others.

Fractions   Fraksyon

one quarter / one fourth	one third	one half / half	two thirds	three quarters / three fourths

A. Is this on sale?
B. Yes. It's _____ off the regular price.

A. Is the gas tank almost empty?
B. It's about _____ full.

Percents   Pousantaj

10% ten percent	50% fifty percent	75% seventy-five percent	100% one-hundred percent

A. How did you do on the test?
B. I got _____ percent of the answers right.

A. What's the weather forecast?
B. There's a _____ percent chance of rain.

Types of Math   Kalite matematik

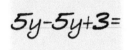 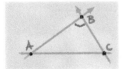 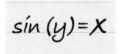 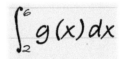 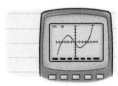

| algebra | geometry | trigonometry | calculus | statistics |
| *aljèb* | *jewometri* | *trigonometri* | *kalkilis* | *statistik* |

A. What math course are you taking this year?
B. I'm taking _____.

Are you good at math?

What math courses do / did you take in school?

Tell about something you bought on sale. How much off the regular price was it?

Research and discuss: What percentage of people in your country live in cities? live on farms? work in factories? vote in general elections?

MEZI AK FÒM JEWOMETRI

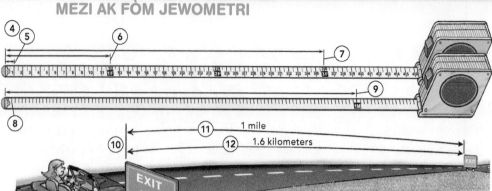
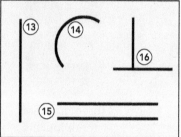
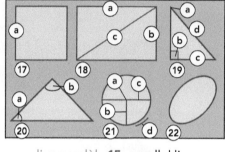
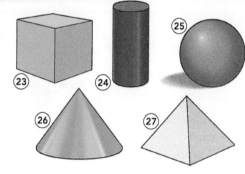

1 mile
1.6 kilometers

EXIT
1 mi.
1.6 km.

Mezi	Measurements
wotè	**1** height
lajè	**2** width
profondè	**3** depth
longè	**4** length
pous	**5** inch
pye-pye	**6** foot–feet
mèt	**7** yard
santimèt	**8** centimeter
mèt	**9** meter
distans	**10** distance
mil	**11** mile
kilomèt	**12** kilometer

Liyn Lines
liyn dwat **13** straight line
liyn koub **14** curved line

liyn paralèl **15** parallel lines
liyn **16** perpendicular
pèpandikilè lines

Fòm Jewometri Geometric Shapes
kare **17** square
kote **a** side
rektang **18** rectangle
longè **a** length
lajè **b** width
dyagonnal **c** diagonal
triyang rektang **19** right triangle
somè **a** apex
ang dwat **b** right angle
baz **c** base
ipoteniz **d** hypotenuse

triyang izosèl **20** isosceles triangle
ang egi **a** acute angle
ang obti **b** obtuse angle
sèk **21** circle
sant **a** center
reyon **b** radius
dyamèt **c** diameter
sikonferans **d** circumference
elip/oval **22** ellipse/oval

Fòm Solid Solid Figures
kib **23** cube
silend **24** cylinder
esfè **25** sphere
kòn **26** cone
piramid **27** pyramid

1 inch (1") = 2.54 centimeters (cm)
1 foot (1') = 0.305 meters (m)
1 yard (1 yd.) = 0.914 meters (m)
1 mile (mi.) = 1.6 kilometers (km)

[1–9]
A. What's the ___[1–4]___?
B. .... ___[5–9]___ (s).

[11–12]
A. What's the distance?
B. .... _____(s).

[17–22]
A. Who can tell me what shape this is?
B. I can. It's a/an _____.

[23–27]
A. Who knows what figure this is?
B. I do. It's a/an _____.

[13–27]
A. This painting is magnificent!
B. Hmm. I don't think so. It just looks like a lot of _____s and _____s to me!

LANG ANGLE AK KONPOZISYON

Types of Sentences & Parts of Speech   Kalite Fraz Ak Pati Diskou

A *Students study in the new library.*
(1)   (2)   (3)   (4)   (5)

C *Read page nine.*

B *Do they study hard?*
(6)   (7)

D *This cake is fantastic!*

fraz deklare	**A** declarative	
enterogativ	**B** interrogative	
fraz kòmande	**C** imperative	
fraz eksklamantwa	**D** exclamatory	

non	**1** noun	
vèb	**2** verb	
prepozisyon	**3** preposition	
atik	**4** article	

adjektiv	**5** adjective	
pwonon	**6** pronoun	
advèb	**7** adverb	

A. What type of sentence is this?
B. It's a/an ___[A–D]___ sentence.

A. What part of speech is this?
B. It's a/an ___[1–7]___.

Punctuation Marks & the Writing Process   Siy Pontiyasyon Ak Pwosesis Redaksyon

pwen	**8** period	
pwen dentèwogasyon	**9** question mark	
pwen desklamasyon	**10** exclamation point	
vigil	**11** comma	
apostwòf	**12** apostrophe	
gimè	**13** quotation marks	
depwen	**14** colon	
pwen vigil	**15** semi-colon	

brase lide	**16** brainstorm ideas	
òganize lide	**17** organize *my* ideas	
ekri yon premye kopi	**18** write a first draft	
tit	**a** title	
paragraf	**b** paragraph	
fè koreksyon	**19** make corrections/revise/edit	
bay fidbak	**20** get feedback	
ekri yon dènnye kopi	**21** write a final copy/rewrite	

A. Did you find any mistakes?
B. Yes. You forgot to put a/an ___[8–15]___ in this sentence.

A. Are you working on your composition?
B. Yes. I'm ___[16–21]___ing.

LITERATI AK EKRI

fiksyon/ istwa imajine	**1** fiction	
woman	**2** novel	
ti istwa	**3** short story	
poem/powèm	**4** poetry/poems	
istwa vre	**5** non-fiction	
byografi	**6** biography	
otobyografi	**7** autobiography	
redaksyon	**8** essay	
rapò	**9** report	
atik magazin	**10** magazine article	
atik jounal	**11** newspaper article	
editoryal	**12** editorial	
lèt	**13** letter	
kat postal	**14** postcard	
nòt	**15** note	
envitasyon	**16** invitation	
lèt remèsiman	**17** thank-you note	
memo	**18** memo	
imèl	**19** e-mail	
mesaj enstantàne	**20** instant message	

A. What are you doing?

B. I'm writing {
    [1, 4, 5].
    a/an _____ [2, 3, 6–20].
}

What kind of literature do you like to read?
What are some of your favorite books?
Who is your favorite author?

Do you like to read newspapers and magazines? Which ones do you read?

Do you sometimes send or receive letters, postcards, notes, e-mail, or instant messages? Tell about the people you communicate with, and how.

JEWOGRAFI

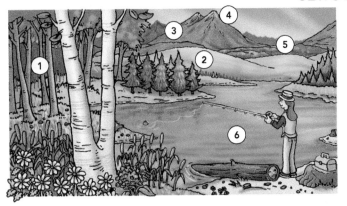

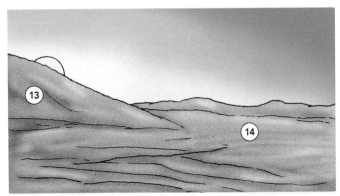

forè/bwa	**1**	forest/woods
ti mòn	**2**	hill
yon gwoup mòn	**3**	mountain range
pwen tèt mòn	**4**	mountain peak
vale	**5**	valley
lak	**6**	lake
plèn yo	**7**	plains
savann	**8**	meadow

ti kouran dlo	**9**	stream/brook
letan	**10**	pond
plato	**11**	plateau
kannyon	**12**	canyon
mòn sab	**13**	dune/sand dune
dezè	**14**	desert
rakbwa	**15**	jungle
bò lanmè	**16**	seashore/shore

bè	**17**	bay
lanmè	**18**	ocean
zile	**19**	island
prèskil	**20**	peninsula
fore	**21**	rainforest
rivyè	**22**	river
chit dlo/kaskad	**23**	waterfall

A. { Isn't this a beautiful _____?!
{ Aren't these beautiful _____s?!

B. Yes. It's / They're magnificent!

Tell about the geography of your country.
Describe the different geographic features.

Have you seen some of the geographic
features in this lesson? Which ones? Where?

SYANS

Ekipman Syantifik	**Science Equipment**		silend ki gen mezi	**12 graduated cylinder**
mikwoskòp	**1** microscope		leman	**13** magnet
konpitè	**2** computer		pris	**14** prism
mòso glas mete nan mikwoskòp	**3** slide		konngout	**15** dropper
ti asyèt plastik nan labowatwa	**4** Petri dish		pwodui chimik	**16** chemicals
			balans	**17** balance
			balans	**18** scale
flas	**5** flask			
antonwa	**6** funnel		**Methòd Syantifik La**	**The Scientific Method**
gòde	**7** beaker		di pwoblèm la	**A** state the problem
tib pou fè tès/egzamen	**8** test tube		fòme yon ipotèz	**B** form a hypothesis
pens	**9** forceps		planifye yon pwosedi	**C** plan a procedure
ti pens	**10** crucible tongs		fè yon pwosedi	**D** do a procedure
Fou a gaz	**11** Bunsen burner		make obzèvasyon	**E** make/record observations
			fè konklizyon	**F** draw conclusions

A. What do we need to do this procedure?
B. We need a/an/the _____ [1–18].

A. How is your experiment coming along?
B. I'm getting ready to _____ [A–F].

Do you have experience with the scientific equipment in this lesson? Tell about it.

What science courses do/did you take in school?

Think of an idea for a science experiment.
What question about science do you want to answer? State the problem.
What do you think will happen in the experiment? Form a hypothesis.
How can you test your hypothesis? Plan a procedure.

LESPAS/LINIVÈ A

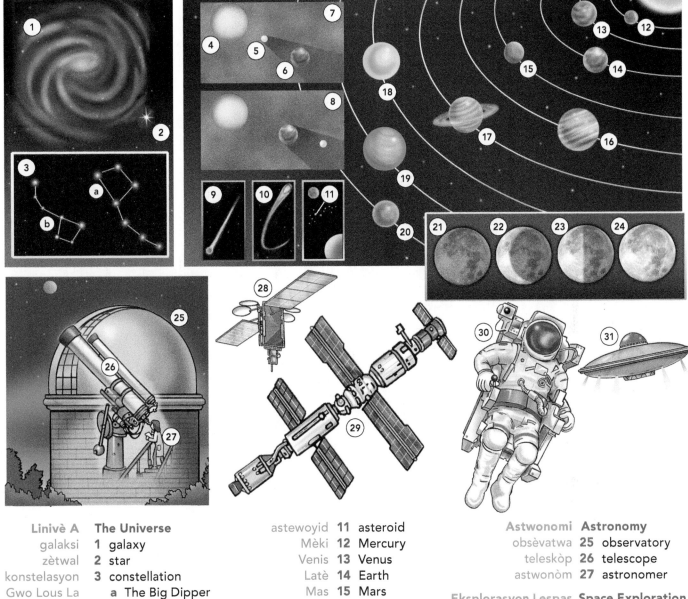

Linivè A		The Universe
galaksi	**1**	galaxy
zètwal	**2**	star
konstelasyon	**3**	constellation
Gwo Lous La	**a**	The Big Dipper
Ti Lous La	**b**	The Little Dipper
Sistèm Solèy		**The Solar System**
solèy	**4**	sun
lalin	**5**	moon
planèt	**6**	planet
eklips solèy	**7**	solar eclipse
eklips lalin	**8**	lunar eclipse
meteyò	**9**	meteor
konmèt	**10**	comet

astewoyid	**11**	asteroid
Mèki	**12**	Mercury
Venis	**13**	Venus
Latè	**14**	Earth
Mas	**15**	Mars
Jipitè	**16**	Jupiter
Satin	**17**	Saturn
Iranis	**18**	Uranus
Neptin	**19**	Neptune
Plito	**20**	Pluto
nouvèl lin	**21**	new moon
kwason lalin	**22**	crescent moon
ka lalin	**23**	quarter moon
lalin antyè	**24**	full moon

Astwonomi		Astronomy
obsèvatwa	**25**	observatory
teleskòp	**26**	telescope
astwonòm	**27**	astronomer
Eksplorasyon Lespas		**Space Exploration**
satelit	**28**	satellite
estasyon nan lespas	**29**	space station
astwonòt	**30**	astronaut
U.F.O./	**31**	U.F.O./
soukoup volan		Unidentified Flying Object/ flying saucer

[1–24]
A. Is that (a/an/the) _____?
B. I'm not sure. I think it might be (a/an/the) _____.

[28–30]
A. Is the _____ ready for tomorrow's launch?
B. Yes. "All systems are go!"

Pretend you are an astronaut traveling in space. What do you see?

Draw and name a constellation you are familiar with.

Do you think space exploration is important? Why?

Have you ever seen a U.F.O.? Do you believe there is life in outer space? Why?

What's the problem?

kontab	1	accountant
aktè	2	actor
aktris	3	actress
achitèk	4	architect
atis pent	5	artist
ajistè	6	assembler
moun ki gade timoun	7	babysitter
boulanje	8	baker
kwafè	9	barber
mason	10	bricklayer/mason
biznismann/komèsan	11	businessman
komèsant	12	businesswoman
machann vyann	13	butcher
chapantye	14	carpenter
kesye	15	cashier
kwizinye	16	chef/cook
anplwaye gadri	17	child day-care worker
enjènyè konpitè	18	computer software engineer
ouvriye nan konstriksyon	19	construction worker
jeran	20	custodian/janitor
reprezantan sèvis kliyan	21	customer service representative
sekretè kap rantre enfòmasyon	22	data entry clerk

gason livrezon	**23**	delivery person	anplwaye nan	**30**	food-service	èd/asistan	**35**	health-care aide/
travayè waf	**24**	dockworker	sèvis manje		worker	enfimyè		attendant
enjenyè	**25**	engineer	kontremèt	**31**	foreman	èd enfimyè	**36**	home health aide/
travayè faktori	**26**	factory worker	jadinye	**32**	gardener/landscaper	nan kay		home attendant
fèmye	**27**	farmer	koutirye/	**33**	garment worker	metrès kay	**37**	homemaker
ponpye	**28**	firefighter	koutiryèz			mennajè	**38**	housekeeper
pechè	**29**	fisher	kwafèz	**34**	hairdresser			

A. What do you do?
B. I'm an **accountant**. How about you?
A. I'm a **carpenter**.

[At a job interview]

A. Are you an experienced _____?
B. Yes. I'm a very experienced _____.

A. How long have you been a/an _____?
B. I've been a/an _____ for
   .... months/years.

Which of these occupations do you think are the most interesting? the most difficult? Why?

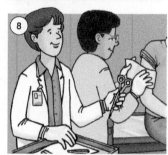

jounalis	**1** journalist/reporter	mizisyen	**11** musician
avoka	**2** lawyer	bòs pent	**12** painter
operatè aparèy	**3** machine operator	famasyen	**13** pharmacist
faktè	**4** mail carrier/letter carrier	fotograf	**14** photographer
manadjè	**5** manager	pilot avyon	**15** pilot
estetisyèn maniki	**6** manicurist	jandam/ajan lapolis	**16** police officer
mekanisyen	**7** mechanic	anplwaye lapòs	**17** postal worker
asistan medikal	**8** medical assistant/ physician assistant	resepsyonis	**18** receptionist
mesaje	**9** messenger/courier	reparatè	**19** repairperson
moun k ap ede demenaje	**10** mover	vandèz/komi magazen	**20** salesperson

travayè vwari	21	sanitation worker/ trash collector	mèt magazen	27	store owner/ shopkeeper	ajan vwayaj	33	travel agent
sekretè	22	secretary				chofè kamyon	34	truck driver
gadyen sekirite	23	security guard	sipèvizè	28	supervisor	veterinè	35	veterinarian/vet
brikolè gason	24	serviceman	tayè	29	tailor	gason	36	waiter/server
brikolè fanm	25	servicewoman	pwofesè/mèt	30	teacher/instructor	madmwazèl	37	waitress/server
anplwaye depo	26	stock clerk	vandè pa telefòn/ telemaketè	31	telemarketer	soudè/wèldè	38	welder
			tradiktè/entèprèt	32	translator/interpreter			

A. What's your occupation?
B. I'm a **journalist**.
A. A **journalist**?
B. Yes. That's right.

A. Are you still a _____?
B. No. I'm a _____.
A. Oh. That's interesting.

A. What kind of job would you like in the future?
B. I'd like to be a _____.

Do you work? What's your occupation?

What are the occupations of people in your family?

KONNESANS TRAVAY AK AKTIVITE

fè teyat	1	act
ajiste pyès/sanble pyès	2	assemble components
ede malad	3	assist patients
anfounen	4	bake
monte/konstwi bagay	5	build things/construct things
netwaye	6	clean
kwit	7	cook
livre pitza	8	deliver pizzas
fè desen batisman	9	design buildings
desinen	10	draw
kondi yon kamyon	11	drive a truck
klase	12	file
pilote yon avyon	13	fly an airplane
plante legim	14	grow vegetables
siveye batisman	15	guard buildings
dirije yon restoran	16	manage a restaurant
koupe gazon	17	mow lawns
travay sou machin	18	operate equipment
pentire	19	paint
jwe pyano	20	play the piano

Por favor complete esto.

Да. Yes.

prepare *manje*	**21**	prepare *food*	okipe *granmoun*	**29** take care of *elderly people*
repare/fiske *bagay*	**22**	repair *things*/fix *things*	konte tout pwovizyon	**30** take inventory
vann *machin*	**23**	sell *cars*	anseye	**31** teach
sèvi *manje*	**24**	serve *food*	tradui	**32** translate
koud	**25**	sew	tape	**33** type
chante	**26**	sing	sèvi ak *yon kèsye*	**34** use *a cash register*
pale *Panyòl*	**27**	speak *Spanish*	lave *vesèl*	**35** wash *dishes*
sipèvisè *moun*	**28**	supervise *people*	ekri	**36** write

A. Can you **act**?
B. Yes, I can.

A. Do you know how to _____?
B. Yes. I've been _____ing for years.

A. Tell me about your skills.
B. I can _____, and I can _____.

Tell about your job skills.
What can you do?

CHÈCHE TRAVAY

Diferan kalite anons pou travay/djòb	Types of Job Ads
siy pou travay	**1** help wanted sign
anons pou djòb/ travay	**2** job notice/ job announcement
anons ki klase	**3** classified ad/want ad

Anons travay abrejions	Job Ad Abbreviations
travay tout tan	**4** full-time
travay enpetan	**5** part-time
lib	**6** available
è	**7** hour
Lendi a Vandredi	**8** Monday through Friday
aswè	**9** evenings
anvan	**10** previous
eksperyans	**11** experience
egzije	**12** required
ekselan	**13** excellent

Sèche travay	Job Search
reponn yon anons	**A** respond to an ad
mande enfòmasyon	**B** request information
mande yon antrevi	**C** request an interview
prepare yon dosye/rezime	**D** prepare a resume
abiye byen	**E** dress appropriately
ranpli yon aplikasyon	**F** fill out an application (form)
ale nan yon antrevi	**G** go to an interview
pale osijè sa ou konnen ak kalifikasyon ou	**H** talk about your skills and qualifications
pale osijè eksperyans ou	**I** talk about your experience
mande salè a	**J** ask about the salary
mande kesyon sou benefis yo	**K** ask about the benefits
ekri yon lèt remèsiman	**L** write a thank-you note
gen travay la	**M** get hired

A. How did you find your job?
B. I found it through a ___[1–3]___ .

A. How was your job interview?
B. It went very well.
A. Did you ___[D–F, H–M]___ ?
B. Yes, I did.

Tell about a job you are familiar with. What are the skills and qualifications required for the job? What are the hours? What is the salary?

Tell about how people you know found their jobs.

Tell about your own experience with a job search or a job interview.

KOTE MOUN TRAVAY

saldatant	**A**	reception area	aparèy tenm	**7**	postage meter	bòs	**21**	employer/boss

saldatant **A** reception area
sal konferans **B** conference room
sal pou triye lèt **C** mailroom
kote moun travay **D** work area
biwo **E** office
sal founiti **F** supply room
sal depo **G** storage room
sal anplwaye **H** employee lounge
pòt manto **1** coat rack
plaka manto **2** coat closet
resepsyonis **3** receptionist
tab konferans **4** conference table
tablo prezantasyon **5** presentation board
balans lapòs **6** postal scale

aparèy tenm **7** postage meter
asistan biwo **8** office assistant
kazye lapòs **9** mailbox
kare travay **10** cubicle
chèz woulant **11** swivel chair
machinaekri **12** typewriter
machin adisyonnen **13** adding machine
machin fotokopi **14** copier/photocopier
aparèy pou filange **15** paper shredder
giyotin **16** paper cutter
achivis **17** file clerk
klasè **18** file cabinet
sekretè **19** secretary
kote moun travay **20** computer workstation
sou konpitè/kare konpitè

bòs **21** employer/boss
asistan administratif **22** administrative assistant
chèf biwo **23** office manager
kabinè founiti **24** supply cabinet
kabinè depo **25** storage cabinet
machin fridòdòy **26** vending machine
aparèy dlo fre **27** water cooler
machin kafe **28** coffee machine
tablo pou mesaj **29** message board
pran yon mesaj **a** take a message
fè yon prezantasyon **b** give a presentation
separe lèt yo **c** sort the mail
fè kopi **d** make copies
katab **e** file
tape yon lèt **f** type a letter

[A–H]
A. Where's ....(name)....... ?
B. He's/She's in the _____.

[1–29]
A. What do you think of the new _____?
B. He's/She's/It's very nice.

[a–f]
A. What's ....(name)....... doing?
B. He's/She's _____ing.

Describe a workplace you are familiar with. Tell about the rooms, the areas, and the employees.

FOUNITI NAN BIWO AK EKIPMAN

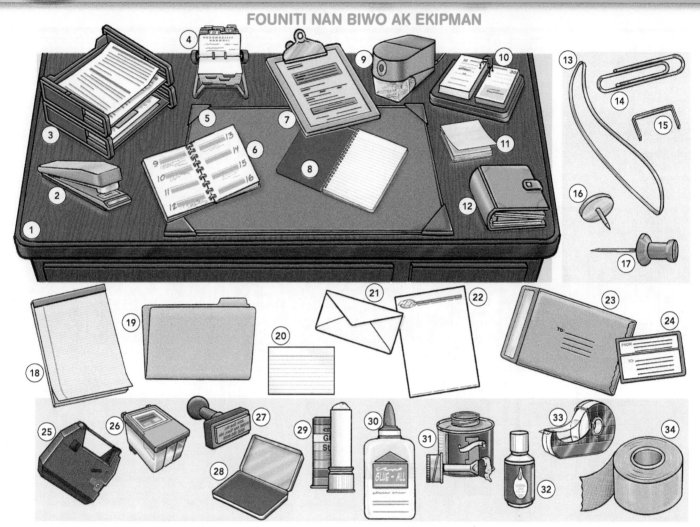

biwo	**1**	desk
agrafèz	**2**	stapler
plato	**3**	letter tray/
lèt		stacking tray
wolodèks	**4**	rotary card file
soumen	**5**	desk pad
liv	**6**	appointment
randevou		book
ekritwa	**7**	clipboard
kaye	**8**	note pad/
nòt		memo pad
tay kreyon	**9**	electric pencil
elektrik		sharpener
almannak biwo	**10**	desk calendar
papye	**11**	Post-It note
kolan		pad

kanè	**12**	organizer/
pèsonnèl		personal planner
elastik	**13**	rubber band
klip metal	**14**	paper clip
agraf	**15**	staple
pinèz	**16**	thumbtack
pinèz ak tèt	**17**	pushpin
blòk papye jòn	**18**	legal pad
katab	**19**	file folder
kat endèks	**20**	index card
anvlòp	**21**	envelope
antèt/	**22**	stationery/
papye		letterhead
lèt		(paper)
anvlòp lapòs	**23**	mailer
etikèt adrès	**24**	mailing label

flakon pou	**25**	typewriter
machinaekri		cartridge
flakon lank	**26**	ink cartridge
pou konpitè		
so	**27**	rubber stamp
tanpon lank	**28**	ink pad
baton lakòl	**29**	glue stick
lakòl	**30**	glue
lakòl	**31**	rubber
PVC		cement
likid pou efase	**32**	correction fluid
tep fen/klè pou	**33**	cellophane tape/
sèvis biwo		clear tape
tep	**34**	packing tape/
anbalaj		sealing tape

A. My desk is a mess!
  I can't find my __[2–12]__ !
B. Here it is next to your __[2–12]__ .

A. Could you get some more
  __[13–21, 23–29]__ s / __[22, 30–34]__
  from the supply room?
B. Some more __[13–21, 23–29]__ s /
  __[22, 30–34]__ ? Sure. I'd be happy to.

Which supplies and equipment do you use?
What do you use them for?

Which supplies in this lesson do you have at home? at school?

FABRIK LA

pandil prezans	**1**	time clock	machin	**9**	machine	depatman	**17**	shipping department
kat lè	**2**	time cards	tapi woulant	**10**	conveyor belt	ekspedisyon		
vestyè	**3**	locker room	depo	**11**	warehouse	anplwaye	**18**	shipping clerk
chenn asanblaj	**4**	(assembly) line	anbalè	**12**	packer	ekspedisyon	**19**	hand truck/ dolly
travayè faktori	**5**	(factory) worker	machin transpò	**13**	forklift	charyo		
estasyon travay	**6**	work station	koli lou	**14**	freight elevator	platfòm chajman	**20**	loading dock
sipèvizè liyn	**7**	line supervisor	elevatè machandiz			biwo pewòl	**21**	payroll office
sipèvizè kalite	**8**	quality control supervisor	tablo nòt sendika	**15**	union notice	biwo pèsonnèl	**22**	personnel office
travay			bwat sijesyon	**16**	suggestion box			

A. Excuse me. I'm a new employee. Where's / Where are the _____?
B. Next to / Near / In / On the _____.

A. Have you seen *Tony*?
B. Yes. *He's* in / on / at / next to / near the _____.

Are there any factories where you live? What kind? What are the working conditions there?

What products do factories in your country produce?

KOTE Y AP BATI

mato mas	**1**	sledgehammer	echafo	**12**	scaffolding	fèy panno	**22**	drywall

mato mas **1** sledgehammer
pikwa **2** pickax
pèl **3** shovel
bourèt **4** wheelbarrow
mato **5** jackhammer/
konpresè pneumatic drill
plan batisman **6** blueprints
nechèl **7** ladder
riban mezi **8** tape measure
senti zouti **9** toolbelt
tiwèl **10** trowel
malaksè **11** cement
 mixer
siman **a** cement

echafo **12** scaffolding
kamyon baskil **13** dump truck
lodè **14** front-end
 loader
machin elevatè **15** crane
machin elevatè **16** cherry
travayè picker
bouldozè **17** bulldozer
pèl mekanik **18** backhoe
malaksè **19** concrete
 mixer truck
beton **a** concrete
pikòp **20** pickup truck
trelè **21** trailer

fèy panno **22** drywall
bwa/planch **23** wood/lumber
playwoud **24** plywood
izolan **25** insulation
fil elektrik **26** wire
brik **27** brick
chingèl **28** shingle
fè tiyo **29** pipe
pout metal **30** girder/beam

A. Could you get me that/those
   ___[1–10]___ ?
B. Sure.

A. Watch out for that ____[11–21]____ !
B. Oh! Thanks for the warning!

A. Do we have enough
   ___[22–26]___ / ___[27–30]___ s?
B. I think so.

What building materials is your home made of?
When was it built?

Describe a construction site near your home or school.
Tell about the construction equipment and the materials.

PWOTÈJ NAN TRAVAY

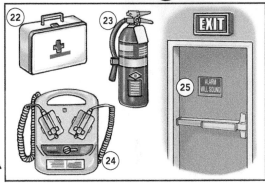

kas pou pwoteje	1	hard hat/ helmet
bouchon zòrèy	2	earplugs
linèt pou pwoteje	3	goggles
vès pwotèj	4	safety vest
bòt pwotèj	5	safety boots
pwoteksyon zòtèy	6	toe guard
sipò do	7	back support
pwotèj zòrèy	8	safety earmuffs
filè	9	hairnet
mask	10	mask
gan latèks	11	latex gloves
respiratè	12	respirator
linèt pou pwoteje	13	safety glasses
ka pran dife	14	flammable
pwazon	15	poisonous
kowozif	16	corrosive
radyoaktiv	17	radioactive
danje	18	dangerous
danje	19	hazardous
danje chimik	20	biohazard
danje elektrik	21	electrical hazard
bwat prenmye swen	22	first-aid kit
ekstentè	23	fire extinguisher
defibrilatè	24	defibrillator
pòtsekoui/ sòti ijans	25	emergency exit

DANGER

CAUTION HAZARDOUS AREA

EXIT ALARM WILL SOUND

A. Don't forget to wear your ___[1–13]___!
B. Thanks for reminding me.

A. Be careful!
- That material is ___[14–17]___!
- That machine is ___[18]___!
- That work area is ___[19]___!
- That's a ___[20]___!/That's an ___[21]___!

B. Thanks for the warning.

A. Where's the ___[22–25]___?
B. It's over there.

Have you ever used any of the safety equipment in this lesson?
What have you used? When? Where?

Where do you see people using safety equipment in your community?

TRANSPÒ PIBLIK

bis	A	bus
estòp bis	1	bus stop
wout bis	2	bus route
pasaje	3	passenger/rider
lajan otobis	4	(bus) fare
transfè	5	transfer
chofè bis	6	bus driver
estasyon bis	7	bus station
kontwa gichè	8	ticket counter
tikè	9	ticket
konpatman / malèt	10	baggage compartment/ luggage compartment

tren	B	train
estasyon tren	11	train station
gichè/fenèt tikè	12	ticket window
tablo arrive ak sòti	13	arrival and departure board
gichè enfòmasyon	14	information booth
orè	15	schedule/ timetable
platfòm	16	platform
ray	17	track
chofè tren	18	conductor

sòbwe	C	subway
estasyon sòbwe	19	subway station
tokenn sòbwe	20	(subway) token
pasaj sou platfòm	21	turnstile
kat sòbwe	22	fare card
machin kat sòbwe	23	fare card machine
taksi	D	taxi
estasyon taksi	24	taxi stand
taksi	25	taxi/cab/taxicab
kontè	26	meter
chofè taksi	27	cab driver/taxi driver
bato navèt	E	ferry

[A–E]
A. How are you going to get there?
B. { I'm going to take the __[A–C, E]__ .
{ I'm going to take a __[D]__ .

[1, 7, 8, 10–19, 21, 23–25]
A. Excuse me. Where's the _____?
B. Over there.

How do you get to different places in your community? Describe public transportation where you live.

In your country, can you travel far by train or by bus? Where can you go? How much do tickets cost? Describe the buses and trains.

DIFERAN KALITE MACHIN

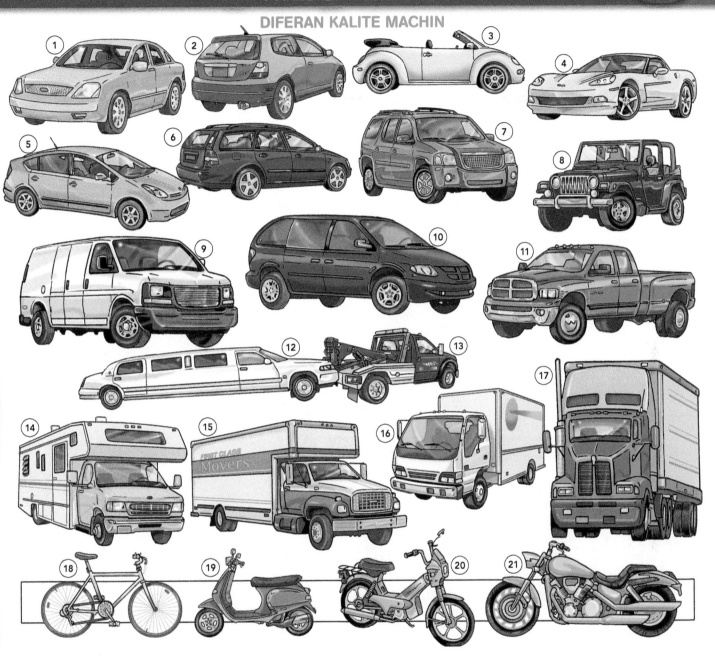

vwati	**1** sedan	jip	**8** jeep	kamyon demenaje	**15** moving van
vwati hatchbak	**2** hatchback	venn	**9** van	kamyon	**16** truck
dekapotab	**3** convertible	minivenn	**10** minivan	trelè	**17** tractor trailer/semi
machin de kous	**4** sports car	kamyon pikòp	**11** pickup truck	bisiklèt	**18** bicycle/bike
ibrid/machin san gaz	**5** hybrid	limouzin	**12** limousine	velomotè	**19** motor scooter
gwo vwati	**6** station wagon	remòk	**13** tow truck	twotinèt a motè	**20** moped
katpakat	**7** S.U.V. (sport utility vehicle)	woulòt	**14** R.V. (recreational vehicle)/camper	motosiklèt	**21** motorcycle

A. What kind of vehicle are you looking for?
B. I'm looking for a **sedan**.

A. Do you drive a/an _____?
B. No. I drive a/an _____.

A. I just saw an accident between a/an _____ and a/an _____!
B. Was anybody hurt?
A. No. Fortunately, nobody was hurt.

What are the most common types of vehicles in your country?

What's your favorite type of vehicle? Why? In your opinion, which company makes the best one?

PATI MACHIN AK SWEN

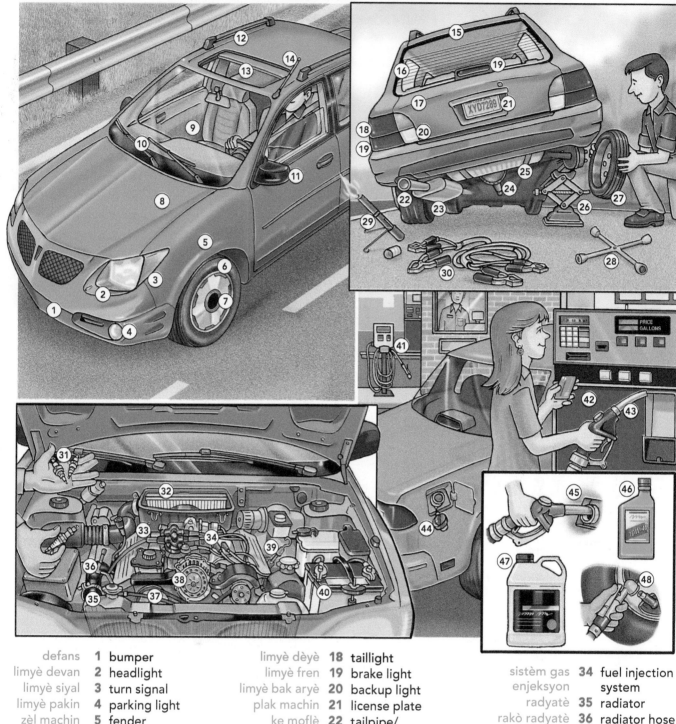

defans	**1**	bumper	limyè dèyè	**18**	taillight	
limyè devan	**2**	headlight	limyè fren	**19**	brake light	
limyè siyal	**3**	turn signal	limyè bak aryè	**20**	backup light	
limyè pakin	**4**	parking light	plak machin	**21**	license plate	
zèl machin	**5**	fender	ke moflè	**22**	tailpipe/	
kawotchou	**6**	tire			exhaust pipe	
kapo wou	**7**	hubcap	mòflè	**23**	muffler	
kapo mote	**8**	hood	transmisyon	**24**	transmission	
vit machin	**9**	windshield	tank gaz	**25**	gas tank	
eswi glas	**10**	windshield	djak	**26**	jack	
		wipers	kawotchou	**27**	spare tire	
retwovizè	**11**	side mirror	derechanj			
pòt bagay	**12**	roof rack	kle wou	**28**	lug wrench	
twati louvri	**13**	sunroof	siyal aksidan	**29**	flare	
antèn	**14**	antenna	kab	**30**	jumper cables	
vit dèyè	**15**	rear window	bouji	**31**	spark plugs	
deglasè	**16**	rear defroster	filtè van	**32**	air filter	
kòf	**17**	trunk	motè machin	**33**	engine	

sistèm gaz enjeksyon	**34**	fuel injection system
radyatè	**35**	radiator
rakò radyatè	**36**	radiator hose
sentiwon vantilatè	**37**	fan belt
altènatè	**38**	alternator
mezi luil/mezi lwil	**39**	dipstick
batri	**40**	battery
ponp van	**41**	air pump
ponp gaz	**42**	gas pump
bouch ponp gaz	**43**	nozzle
bouchon gaz	**44**	gas cap
gaz	**45**	gas
luil/lwil	**46**	oil
antifriz	**47**	coolant
lè	**48**	air

sak van	**49**	air bag	sistèm navigasyon	**63**	navigation system	chanjman vitès otomatik	**75**	gearshift
vizyè	**50**	visor	radyo	**64**	radio	transmisyon ak men	**76**	manual transmission
retwovizè	**51**	rearview mirror	jwè CD	**65**	CD player	chanjman vitès ak men	**77**	stickshift
dachbòd	**52**	dashboard/ instrument panel	chofaj	**66**	heater	klòtch	**78**	clutch
kadran tanperati	**53**	temperature gauge	kilmatizè èkondisyone	**67**	air conditioning	seri pòt	**79**	door lock
kadran gaz	**54**	gas gauge/fuel gauge	deglasè	**68**	defroster	manch pòt	**80**	door handle
spidomèt	**55**	speedometer	priz kouran	**69**	power outlet	senti	**81**	shoulder harness
odomèt	**56**	odometer	kòf	**70**	glove compartment	sekirite zepòl		
limyè avètisman	**57**	warning lights	fren ijans	**71**	emergency brake	apui bra	**82**	armrest
limyè siyal	**58**	turn signal	pedal fren	**72**	brake (pedal)	apui tèt	**83**	headrest
volan	**59**	steering wheel	akseleratè/ pedal gaz	**73**	accelerator/ gas pedal	chèz	**84**	seat
klaksòn	**60**	horn	transmisyon otomatik	**74**	automatic transmission	senti sekirite	**85**	seat belt
switch machin	**61**	ignition						
twou van	**62**	vent						

[2, 3, 9–16, 24, 35–39, 49–85]
A. What's the matter with your car?
B. The _____(s) is/are broken.

[45–48]
A. Can I help you?
B. { Yes. My car needs [45–47]. / Yes. My tires need [48]. }

[1, 2, 4–15, 17–23, 25]
A. I was just in a car accident!
B. Oh, no! Were you hurt?
A. No. But my _____(s) was/were damaged.

In your opinion, what are the most important features to look for when you buy a car?

Do you own a car? What kind? Tell about any repairs your car has needed.

GRAN WOUT AK LARI

tinèl	**1**	tunnel	gran wout	**11**	interstate	panno siyal sòti	**21**	exit sign
pon	**2**	bridge	ant eta		(highway)	lari	**22**	street
kabin peyaj	**3**	tollbooth	separasyon	**12**	median	risans inik	**23**	one-way
siyal wout	**4**	route sign	liy agòch	**13**	left lane			street
gran wout	**5**	highway	liy nan mitan	**14**	middle lane/	liy jòn doub	**24**	double
wout	**6**	road			center lane			yellow line
separasyon/	**7**	divider/	liy adwat	**15**	right lane	pasaj pyeton	**25**	crosswalk
baryè siman		barrier	zòn estasyonnman	**16**	shoulder	kafou	**26**	intersection
wout anwo	**8**	overpass	liy kase	**17**	broken line	limyè	**27**	traffic light/
wout anba	**9**	underpass	liy solid	**18**	solid line	sikilasyon		traffic signal
ranp pou rantre/	**10**	entrance ramp/	panno limit	**19**	speed limit	kwen	**28**	corner
gran wout		on ramp	vitès		sign	blòk	**29**	block
			ranp pou sòti	**20**	exit (ramp)			

[1–28]

A. Where's the accident?

B. It's on / in / at / near the _____.

Describe a highway you travel on.

Describe an intersection near where you live.

In your area, on which highways and streets do most accidents occur? Why are these places dangerous?

PREPOZISYON MOUVMAN

  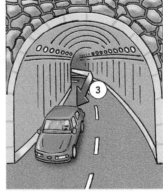 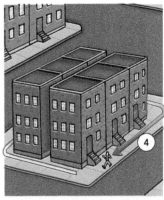

anwo	**1**	over
annsou	**2**	under
pase nan	**3**	through
around	**4**	around

anwo	**5**	up
anba	**6**	down
atravè	**7**	across
pase	**8**	past

sou	**9**	on
etenn/kanpe lwen	**10**	off
nan	**11**	into
deyò	**12**	out of
nan	**13**	onto

[1–8]
A. Go **over** the bridge.
B. **Over** the bridge?
A. Yes.

[9–13]
A. I can't talk right now. I'm getting **on** a train.
B. You're getting **on** a train?
A. Yes. I'll call you later.

What places do you go past on your way to school?   Tell how to get to different places from your home or your school.

SIY SIKILASYON AK DIREKSYON

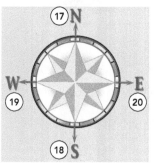  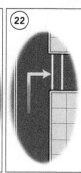 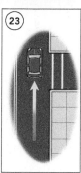  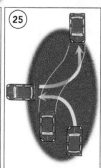 

Siy Sikilasyon		Traffic Signs
rete	1	stop
pa vire agoch	2	no left turn
pa vire adwat	3	no right turn
pa kase tèt tounen	4	no U-turn
vire dwat sèlman	5	right turn only
pa rantre	6	do not enter
sans inik	7	one way
enpas	8	dead end/no outlet
pyeton ap travèse	9	pedestrian crossing
tren kap travèse	10	railroad crossing
travase lekòl	11	school crossing
wout la kontre	12	merging traffic

kite lòt machin pase	13	yield
detou	14	detour
li glise lè li mouye	15	slippery when wet
pakin pou moun andikape sèlman	16	handicapped parking only

Direksyon bousòl		Compass Directions
nò	17	north
sid	18	south
wès	19	west
ès	20	east

Entriksyon Apran Kondwi		Road Test Instructions
Vire agoch.	21	Turn left.
Vire adwat.	22	Turn right.
Al dwat.	23	Go straight.
Pakin paralèl.	24	Parallel park.
Fè yon vire a twa pwen.	25	Make a 3-point turn.
Sèvi ak siyal men.	26	Use hand signals.

[1–16]
A. Careful! That sign says "**stop**"!
B. Oh. Thanks.

[17–20]
A. Which way should I go?
B. Go **north**.

[21–26]
A. Turn **right**.
B. Turn **right**?
A. Yes.

Which of these traffic signs are in your neighborhood?
What other traffic signs do you usually see?

Describe any differences between traffic signs in different countries you know.

AYEWOPÒ A

Anrejistreman	**A**	**Check-In**
tikèt	**1**	ticket
kontwa tikèt	**2**	ticket counter
ajan tikèt	**3**	ticket agent
malèt	**4**	suitcase
ekran rive ak depa	**5**	arrival and departure monitor
Sekirite	**B**	**Security**
estasyon sekirite	**6**	security checkpoint
detektè metal	**7**	metal detector
ofisye sekirite	**8**	security officer
aparèy radyografi	**9**	X-ray machine
sakamen	**10**	carry-on bag

Pòt depa	**C**	**The Gate**
kontwa anrejistreman	**11**	check-in counter
kat pasaj	**12**	boarding pass
pòt depa	**13**	gate
zòn pasaj	**14**	boarding area
Reklamasyon Bagaj	**D**	**Baggage Claim**
zòn reklamasyon bagaj	**15**	baggage claim (area)
charyo	**16**	baggage carousel
bagaj	**17**	baggage
charyo bagaj	**18**	baggage cart/ luggage cart
pòtbagaj	**19**	luggage carrier
sak pandri	**20**	garment bag
tikèt bagaj	**21**	baggage claim check

Ladwann ak Imigrasyon	**E**	**Customs and Immigration**
ladwann	**22**	customs
anplwaye ladwann	**23**	customs officer
fòm deklarasyon ladwann	**24**	customs declaration form
imigrasyon	**25**	immigration
anplwaye imigrasyon	**26**	immigration officer
paspò	**27**	passport
viza	**28**	visa

[2, 3, 5–9, 11, 13–16, 22, 23, 25, 26]
A. Excuse me. Where's the _____?*
B. Right over there.

* With 22 and 25 use: Excuse me. Where's _____?

[1, 4, 10, 12, 17–21, 24, 27, 28]
A. Oh, no! I think I've lost my _____!
B. I'll help you look for it.

Describe an airport you are familiar with. Tell about the check-in area, the security area, the gates, and the baggage claim area.

Have you ever gone through Customs and Immigration? Tell about your experience.

VWAYAJE NAN AVYON

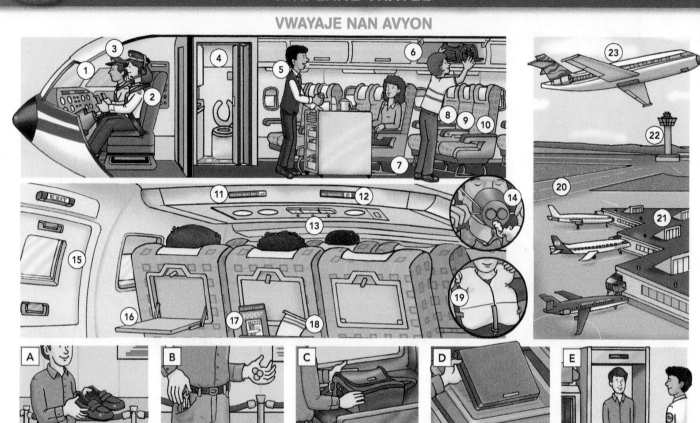

kòkpit	**1**	cockpit
pilot/kaptenn	**2**	pilot/captain
dezyèm pilòt	**3**	co-pilot
lavabo/twalèt	**4**	lavatory/bathroom
otès avyon	**5**	flight attendant
konpatiman	**6**	overhead compartment
ale	**7**	aisle
fotèy fennèt	**8**	window seat
fotèy mitan	**9**	middle seat
fotèy ale	**10**	aisle seat
siyal boukle senti	**11**	Fasten Seat Belt sign
siyal pa fimen	**12**	No Smoking sign
bouton sonnèt	**13**	call button
mask oksijèn	**14**	oxygen mask
sòti ijans	**15**	emergency exit
plato tab	**16**	tray (table)
kat enfòmasyon pou ijans	**17**	emergency instruction card
sache pou vomi	**18**	air sickness bag

jile sovtaj	**19**	life vest/life jacket
pis aterisaj	**20**	runway
batisman tèminal	**21**	terminal (building)
toudkontwòl	**22**	control tower
avyon	**23**	airplane/plane/jet

retire soulye ou	**A**	take off your shoes
vide pòch ou	**B**	empty your pockets
mete sak ou sou tapi woulan an	**C**	put your bag on the conveyor belt
depoze konpitè w la nan yon plato	**D**	put your computer in a tray
pase anba metal detèktè	**E**	walk through the metal detector
tcheke nan pòt antre a	**F**	check in at the gate
pran fich anbakman	**G**	get your boarding pass
monte nan avyon an	**H**	board the plane
mete sakamen w anba	**I**	stow your carry-on bag
jwenn plas ou	**J**	find your seat
mete sentiwon ou	**K**	fasten your seat belt

[1–23]
A. Where's the _____?
B. In/On/Next to/Behind/In front of/
Above/Below the _____.

[A–K]
A. Please _____.
B. All right. Certainly.

Have you ever flown in an airplane?
Tell about a flight you took.

Be an airport security officer! Give passengers instructions as they go through the security area. Now, be a flight attendant! Give passengers instructions before take-off.

OTÈL LA

pòtyè	**1**	doorman	resepsyonis	**9**	desk clerk	elevatè/asansè	**18**	elevator
sèvis	**2**	valet	gès/envite	**10**	guest	machin ki fè glas	**19**	ice machine
pakin		parking	biwo	**11**	concierge	koulwa	**20**	hall/hallway
moun ki	**3**	parking	konsyèj		desk	kle chanm	**21**	room key
pake machin		attendant	konsyèj	**12**	concierge	bourèt atik	**22**	housekeeping
pòtè	**4**	bellhop	restoran	**13**	restaurant	netwayaj		cart
pòt	**5**	luggage	chanm	**14**	meeting	mennajè	**23**	housekeeper
bagaj		cart	reyinyon		room	chanm pou envite	**24**	guest room
chef pòtè	**6**	bell captain	boutik kado	**15**	gift shop	sèvis manje	**25**	room service
saldatant	**7**	lobby	pisin	**16**	pool			
biwo enskripsyon	**8**	front desk	chanm	**17**	exercise			
			egzèsis		room			

A. Where do you work?
B. I work at the *Grand* Hotel.
A. What do you do there?
B. I'm a/an ____[1, 3, 4, 6, 9, 12, 23]____.

A. Excuse me. Where's the ____[1–19, 22, 23]____?
B. Right over there.
A. Thanks.

Tell about a hotel you are familiar with. Describe the place and the people.

In your opinion, which hotel employee has the most interesting job? the most difficult job? Why?

OUVRAJ, PASTAN AK JWÈT

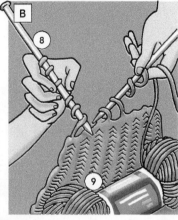
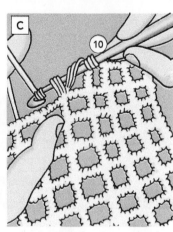
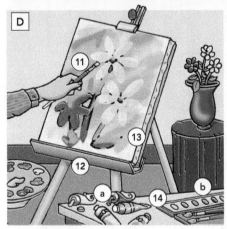
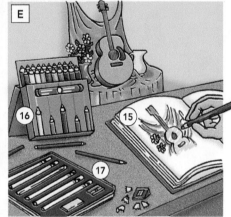
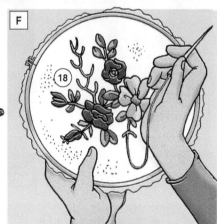
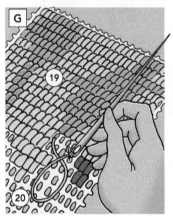

koud	**A**	**sew**
machinakoud	**1**	sewing machine
zepeng	**2**	pin
plot zepeng	**3**	pin cushion
fil	**4**	(spool of) thread
zegwi	**5**	(sewing) needle
de pou kouti	**6**	thimble
zepeng kouchèt	**7**	safety pin

triko	**B**	**knit**
zegwi triko	**8**	knitting needle
plòtfil	**9**	yarn

kwochè	**C**	**crochet**
zegwi kwochè	**10**	crochet hook

penti	**D**	**paint**
bwòs pou fè penti	**11**	paintbrush
trepye	**12**	easel
twal penti	**13**	canvas
penti	**14**	paint
penti aluil		**a** oil paint
penti alo		**b** watercolor

desinen	**E**	**draw**
kaye desen	**15**	sketch book
kreyon koulè	**16**	(set of) colored pencils
kreyon desen	**17**	drawing pencil

fè bwodri	**F**	**do embroidery**
bwodri	**18**	embroidery

fè travay zegwi	**G**	**do needlepoint**
travay zegwi	**19**	needlepoint
desen	**20**	pattern

fè ebenistri	**H**	**do woodworking**
bwat pou ebenistri	**21**	woodworking kit

fè origami	**I**	**do origami**
papye origami	**22**	origami paper

fè potri	**J**	**make pottery**
ajil	**23**	clay
wou potye	**24**	potter's wheel

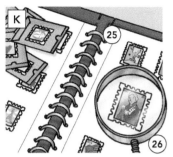

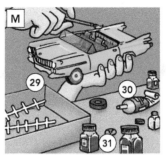

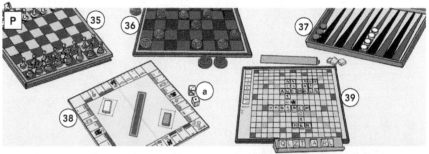

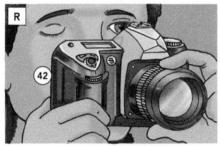

koleksyon tenm	**K**	**collect stamps**
albòm kolèksyon tenm	**25**	stamp album
loup	**26**	magnifying glass
koleksyon monnen	**L**	**collect coins**
katalòg monnen	**27**	coin catalog
albòm monnen	**28**	coin collection
konstwi model	**M**	**build models**
bwat pou modèl	**29**	model kit
lakòl	**30**	glue
penti akrilik	**31**	acrylic paint
ale obzève zwazo	**N**	**go bird-watching**
longvi	**32**	binoculars
gid rejyon	**33**	field guide

jwe kat	**O**	**play cards**
kat	**34**	(deck of) cards
trèf		**a** club
kawo		**b** diamond
kè		**c** heart
pik		**d** spade
jwèt sou tab	**P**	**play board games**
echèk	**35**	chess
damye	**36**	checkers
bakgamon	**37**	backgammon
Monnopoli	**38**	Monopoly
zo		**a** dice
Eskrabèl	**39**	Scrabble

ale nan konpitè a	**Q**	**go online/ browse the Web/ "surf" the net**
chèche nan wèb	**40**	web browser
adrès wèb	**41**	web address/URL
fotografi	**R**	**photography**
kamera/Kodak	**42**	camera
astwonomi	**S**	**astronomy**
teleskòp	**43**	telescope

A. What do you like to do in your free time?
B. { I like to ___[A–Q]___ .
{ I enjoy ___[R, S]___ .

A. May I help you?
B. Yes, please. I'd like to buy (a/an) ___[1–34, 42, 43]___ .

A. What do you want to do?
B. Let's play ___[35–39]___ .
A. Good idea!

Do you like to do any of these activities in your free time? Which ones?

What games are popular in your country? Describe how to play one.

PLAS POU ALE

mize	**1**	museum	mache	**8**	craft fair
galri da	**2**	art gallery	vann pèpè sou gazon/garaj	**9**	yard sale
konsè	**3**	concert	mache	**10**	swap meet/ flea market
pyès teyat	**4**	play	plas	**11**	park
plas rekreyasyon	**5**	amusement park	plaj	**12**	beach
plas istorik	**6**	historic site	mòn	**13**	mountains
plas nasyonal	**7**	national park			

akwaryòm	**14**	aquarium
jaden botanik	**15**	botanical gardens
planetaryòm	**16**	planetarium
zou	**17**	zoo
sinema	**18**	movies
kanaval	**19**	carnival
mache	**20**	fair

A. What do you want to do today?

B. Let's go to { a/an ____[1–9]____. the ____[10–20]____.

A. What did you do over the weekend?

B. I went to { a/an ____[1–9]____. the ____[10–20]____.

A. What are you going to do on your day off?

B. I'm going to go to { a/an ____[1–9]____. the ____[10–20]____.

What are some of your favorite places to go? Where are they? What do you do there?

JADEN AK TEREN POU JWE

wout	**1**	bicycle path/	ban	**9**	bench	teren pou jwe	**16** playground
bisiklèt		bike path/	teren tenis	**10**	tennis court	grenpe mi	**17** climbing wall
		bikeway	teren pou jwe	**11**	ballfield	balanswa	**18** swings
letan kanna	**2**	duck pond	besbòl			moun ki grenpe	**19** climber
zòn piknik	**3**	picnic area	fontenn	**12**	fountain	glisad	**20** slide
poubèl	**4**	trash can	pakin bisiklèt	**13**	bike rack	jwèt baskil	**21** seesaw
griy	**5**	grill	kawousèl	**14**	merry-go-round/	bwat sab	**22** sandbox
tab piknik	**6**	picnic table			carousel	sab	**23** sand
fontenn dlo pou bwè	**7**	water fountain	planchèt awoulèt	**15**	skateboard ramp		
chemen jogin	**8**	jogging path					

[1–22]

A. Excuse me. Does this park have (a) _____?

B. Yes. Right over there.

[17–23]

A. { Be careful on the ___[17–21]___ !
{ Be careful in the ___[22, 23]___ !

B. I will, Dad/Mom.

Describe a park and playground you are familiar with.

siveyan plaj	**1**	lifeguard	chèz plaj	**10**	beach chair	wòch	**20**	rock
chèz siveyan plaj	**2**	lifeguard stand	parasol plaj	**11**	beach umbrella	bwat glas	**21**	cooler
kawotchou	**3**	life preserver	chato sab	**12**	sand castle	chapo solèy	**22**	sun hat
boutik	**4**	snack bar/	ti planch ak woulèt	**13**	boogie board	losyon	**23**	sunscreen/
fridòdòy		refreshment	moun k ap pran	**14**	sunbather	pou		sunblock/
		stand	beny solèy			bloke		suntan
machann	**5**	vendor	linèt solèy	**15**	sunglasses	solèy		lotion
najè	**6**	swimmer	sèvyèt plaj	**16**	(beach) towel	lenn	**24**	(beach)
vag	**7**	wave	balon plaj	**17**	beach ball	plaj		blanket
eski sou dlo	**8**	surfer	planch èski sou dlo	**18**	surfboard	pèl	**25**	shovel
kap	**9**	kite	koki	**19**	seashell/shell	bokit	**26**	pail

[1–26]
A. What a nice beach!
B. It is. Look at all the _____s!

[9–11, 13, 15–18, 21–26]
A. Are you ready for the beach?
B. Almost. I just have to get my _____.

Do you like to go to the beach? Describe your favorite beach. What do you take when you go there?

REKREYAKSYON DEYÒ

kanpin	A	camping
tant	1	tent
sak kouchaj	2	sleeping bag
pikèt tant	3	tent stakes
fannal	4	lantern
rach	5	hatchet
recho kanpin	6	camping stove
kouto	7	Swiss army knife
pwodui pou moustik	8	insect repellent
alimèt	9	matches

mache nan bwa	B	hiking
sakado	10	backpack
kantin	11	canteen
bousòl	12	compass
kat chemen	13	trail map
aparèy GPS	14	GPS device
bòt pou mache nan bwa	15	hiking boots

grenpe wòch	C	rock climbing/ technical climbing
lekisay	16	harness
kòd	17	rope

grenpe mòn	D	mountain biking
bisiklèt mòn	18	mountain bike
kas (bisiklèt)	19	(bike) helmet

piknik	E	picnic
lenn (piknik)	20	(picnic) blanket
tèmòs	21	thermos
panyen piknik	22	picnic basket

A. Let's go ___[A–E]___ * this weekend.
B. Good idea! We haven't gone ___[A–E]___ * in a long time.

*With E, say: on a picnic.

A. Did you bring
{ the ___[1–9, 11–14, 16, 17, 20–22]___ ?
{ your ___[10, 15, 18, 19]___ ?
B. Yes, I did.
A. Oh, good.

Have you ever gone camping, hiking, rock climbing, or mountain biking? Tell about it: What did you do? Where? What equipment did you use?

Do you like to go on picnics? Where? What picnic supplies and food do you take with you?

ESPÒ AK REKREYASYON ENDIVIDYÈL

ti kous modere/jògin	**A jogging**	monte cheval	**H horseback riding**
rad jògin	**1** jogging suit	sèl	**14** saddle
soulye jogin	**2** jogging shoes	renn	**15** reins
		zetriye	**16** stirrups
kous apye	**B running**		
chòt pou kous	**3** running shorts	tennis	**I tennis**
soulye pou kous	**4** running shoes	rakèt tennis	**17** tennis racket
		boul tennis	**18** tennis ball
mache	**C walking**	chòt tennis	**19** tennis shorts
soulye pou mache	**5** walking shoes		
		badmiton	**J badminton**
wolèbledin/patinaj egzibisyon	**D inline skating/rollerblading**	rakèt badmiton	**20** badminton racket
wolèbledin/patinaj egzibisyon	**6** inline skates/rollerblades	bèdi	**21** birdie/shuttlecock
jennouyè	**7** knee pads		
		rakètboul	**K racquetball**
monte bisiklèt	**E cycling/biking**	linèt pwotèj	**22** safety goggles
bisiklèt	**8** bicycle/bike	boul pou jwe rakètboul	**23** racquetball
kas	**9** (bicycle/bike)	rakèt	**24** racquet
(bisiklèt)	helmet		
		pingpong	**L table tennis/**
monte planch ak woulèt	**F skateboarding**		**ping pong**
planch ak woulèt	**10** skateboard	rakèt pingpong	**25** paddle
pwotèj koud	**11** elbow pads	tab pingpong	**26** ping pong table
		file	**27** net
bolin	**G bowling**	boul pingpong	**28** ping pong ball
boul bolin	**12** bowling ball		
soulye bolin	**13** bowling shoes		

gòf	M	golf
baton gòf	29	golf clubs
boul gòf	30	golf ball

frisbi	N	Frisbee
frisbi	31	Frisbee/ flying disc

biya	O	billiards/pool
tab biya	32	pool table
baton biya	33	pool stick
boul biya	34	billiard balls

karate	P	martial arts
senti nwa	35	black belt

jimnastik	Q	gymnastics
chwal	36	horse
ba paralèl	37	parallel bars
matla	38	mat
pout ekilib	39	balance beam
tranplen	40	trampoline

leve fè	R	weightlifting
babèl	41	barbell
pwa	42	weights

tire flèch	S	archery
ak e flèch	43	bow and arrow
sib	44	target

bòks	T	box
gan bòksè	45	boxing gloves
chòt bòksè	46	(boxing) trunks

lit	U	wrestle
inifòm lit	47	wrestling uniform
tapi lit	48	(wrestling) mat

egzèsis	V	work out/exercise
tapi woulant pou egzèsi	49	treadmill
aparèy kannotaj	50	rowing machine
bisiklèt egzèsis	51	exercise bike
ekipman egzèsis	52	universal/ exercise equipment

[A–V]

A. What do you like to do in your free time?

B. { I like to go ___[A–H]___.
I like to play ___[I–O]___.
I like to do ___[P–S]___.
I like to ___[T–V]___. }

[1–52]

A. I really like this/these new _____.

B. It's/They're very nice.

Do you do any of these activities? Which ones? Which are popular in your country?

ESPÒ ANN EKIP

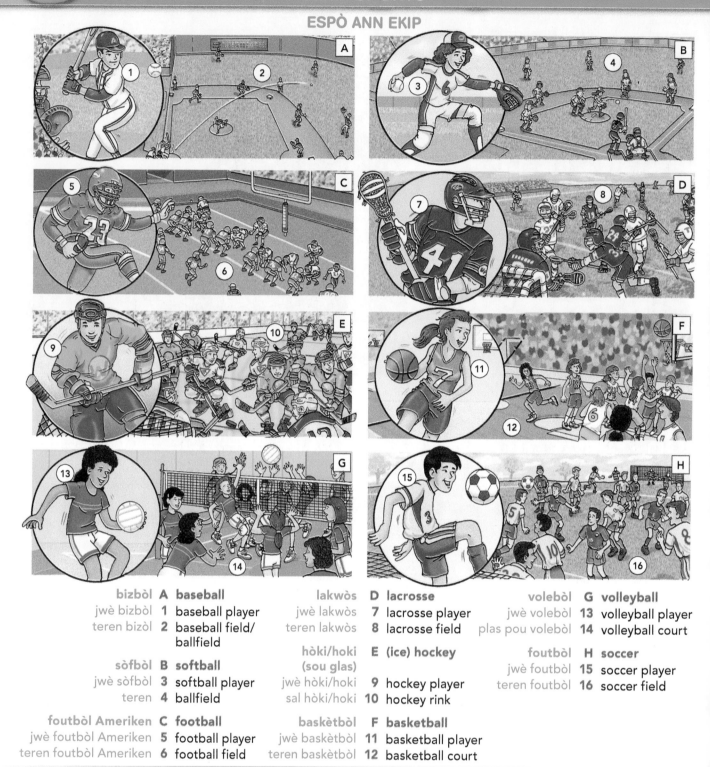

bizbòl	**A**	**baseball**		lakwòs	**D**	**lacrosse**		volebòl	**G**	**volleyball**
jwè bizbòl	**1**	baseball player		jwè lakwòs	**7**	lacrosse player		jwè volebòl	**13**	volleyball player
teren bizòl	**2**	baseball field/ballfield		teren lakwòs	**8**	lacrosse field		plas pou volebòl	**14**	volleyball court
					E	**(ice) hockey**		foutbòl	**H**	**soccer**
sòfbòl	**B**	**softball**		hòki/hoki (sou glas)				jwè foutbòl	**15**	soccer player
jwè sòfbòl	**3**	softball player		jwè hòki/hoki	**9**	hockey player		teren foutbòl	**16**	soccer field
teren	**4**	ballfield		sal hòki/hoki	**10**	hockey rink				
foutbòl Ameriken	**C**	**football**		baskètbòl	**F**	**basketball**				
jwè foutbòl Ameriken	**5**	football player		jwè baskètbòl	**11**	basketball player				
teren foutbòl Ameriken	**6**	football field		teren baskètbòl	**12**	basketball court				

[A–H]
A. Do you like to play **baseball**?
B. Yes. **Baseball** is one of my favorite sports.

A. .... plays __[A–H]__ very well.
B. You're right. I think he's/she's one of the best _____s* on the team.

*Use 1, 3, 5, 7, 9, 11, 13, 15.

A. Now listen, team! I want all of you to go out on that _____† and play the best game of __[A–H]__ you've ever played!
B. All right, Coach!

† Use 2, 4, 6, 8, 10, 12, 14, 16.

Which sports in this lesson do you like to play? Which do you like to watch?

What are your favorite teams?

Name some famous players of these sports.

EKIPMAN POU ESPÒ ANN EKIP

bizbòl	**A**	**baseball**
bal bizbòl	**1**	baseball
baton bizbòl	**2**	bat
chapo bizbòl	**3**	batting helmet
inifòm bizbòl	**4**	(baseball) uniform
mask jwè ki atrape bal la	**5**	catcher's mask
gan bizbòl	**6**	(baseball) glove
gan jwè ki atrape bal la	**7**	catcher's mitt
sòfbòl	**B**	**softball**
bal sòfbòl	**8**	softball
gan sòfbòl	**9**	softball glove

foutbòl Ameriken	**C**	**football**
balon foutbòl	**10**	football
kas foutbòl	**11**	football helmet
pwotèj zepòl	**12**	shoulder pads
lakwòs	**D**	**lacrosse**
bal lakwòs	**13**	lacrosse ball
mas lakwòs	**14**	face guard
rakèt lakwòs	**15**	lacrosse stick
hòki/hoki (sou glas)	**E**	**(ice) hockey**
palèt hòki/hoki	**16**	hockey puck
baton hòki /hoki	**17**	hockey stick
mas hòki/hoki	**18**	hockey mask
gan hòki/hoki	**19**	hockey glove
paten hòki/hoki	**20**	hockey skates

baskètbòl	**F**	**basketball**
balon baskètbòl	**21**	basketball
panno baskètbòl	**22**	backboard
panyen baskètbòl	**23**	basketball hoop
voleból	**G**	**volleyball**
balon voleból	**24**	volleyball
file voleból	**25**	volleyball net
foutbòl asosyasyon	**H**	**soccer**
balon foutbòl	**26**	soccer ball
janbyè pwoteksyon	**27**	shinguards

[1–27]
A. I can't find my **baseball**!
B. Look in the closet.*

*closet, basement, garage

[In a store]
A. Excuse me. I'm looking for (a) __[1–27]__ .
B. All our __[A–H]__ equipment is over there.
A. Thanks.

[At home]
A. I'm going to play __[A–H]__ after school today.
B. Don't forget your __[1–21, 24, 26, 27]__ !

Which sports in this lesson are popular in your country? Which sports do students play in high school?

ESPÒ LIVÈ AK REKREYASYON

eski sou pant	**A**	**(downhill) skiing**
eski	1	skis
bòt eski	2	ski boots
blòk	3	bindings
baton eski	4	(ski) poles
eski sou chemen	**B**	**cross-country skiing**
eski sou chemen	5	cross-country skis

patinay sou glas	**C**	**(ice) skating**
paten	6	(ice) skates
jilè pou paten	7	blade
pwotèj paten	8	skate guard
patinaj egzibisyon	**D**	**figure skating**
paten egzibisyon	9	figure skates
sèfe sou nèj	**E**	**snowboarding**
planch sèfe sou nèj	10	snowboard

glisad nan tren	**F**	**sledding**
treno	11	sled
treno soukoup	12	sledding dish/ saucer
bòbslèdin	**G**	**bobsledding**
bobsled	13	bobsled
kondi machin sou nèj	**H**	**snowmobiling**
machin sou nèj	14	snowmobile

[A–H]
A. What's your favorite winter sport?
B. **Skiing**.

[A–H]
[At work or at school on Friday]
A. What are you going to do this weekend?
B. I'm going to go _____.

[1–14]
[On the telephone]
A. Hello. *Sally's* Sporting Goods.
B. Hello. Do you sell _____(s)?
A. Yes, we do. / No, we don't.

Have you ever done any of these activities? Which ones?

Have you ever watched the Winter Olympics? Which event do you think is the most exciting? the most dangerous?

ESPÒ SOU DLO AK REKREYASYON

navigasyon	**A**	**sailing**
vwalye	**1**	sailboat
jile sovtaj	**2**	life jacket/life vest
kannouin	**B**	**canoeing**
kannou	**3**	canoe
zaviwon	**4**	paddles
kannotaj	**C**	**rowing**
kannòt ak ram	**5**	rowboat
ram	**6**	oars
kayakin	**D**	**kayaking**
kayak	**7**	kayak
page	**8**	paddles
rado sou rivyè	**E**	**(white-water) rafting**
rado gonfle	**9**	raft
jile sovtaj	**10**	life jacket/life vest

naj	**F**	**swimming**
kostimdeben	**11**	swimsuit/bathing suit
linèt pou naje	**12**	goggles
bonnèt pou naje	**13**	bathing cap
plonje anba lanmè	**G**	**snorkeling**
mas pou plonje	**14**	mask
tiyo pou respire	**15**	snorkel
pam pou naje	**16**	fins
plonje nan eskafann	**H**	**scuba diving**
kostim plonje	**17**	wet suit
tank lè	**18**	(air) tank
mas pou plonje	**19**	(diving) mask
glisad sou vag	**I**	**surfing**
planch pou glise	**20**	surfboard

glisadavwal	**J**	**windsurfing**
planchavwal	**21**	sailboard
vwal	**22**	sail
eski sou dlo	**K**	**waterskiing**
eski pou dlo	**23**	water skis
kòd pou rale	**24**	towrope
lapèch	**L**	**fishing**
kannapèch	**25**	(fishing) rod/pole
bobin	**26**	reel
liypou peche	**27**	(fishing) line
filè	**28**	(fishing) net
zen	**29**	bait

[A–L]
A. Would you like to go **sailing** tomorrow?
B. Sure. I'd love to.

A. Have you ever gone ___[A–L]___ ?
B. Yes, I have. / No, I haven't.

A. Do you have everything you need to go ___[A–L]___ ?
B. Yes. I have my ___[1–29]___ (and my ___[1–29]___).
A. Have a good time!

Which sports in this lesson have you tried?
Which sports would you like to try?

Are any of these sports popular in your country? Which ones?

AKTIVITE ESPÒ AK EGZÈSIS

frape	1 hit	drible	9 dribble	sote anlè	17 jump
lanse	2 pitch	lanse	10 shoot	eseye touche anlè	18 reach
voye	3 throw	detire kò	11 stretch		
atrape	4 catch	bese	12 bend	balanse	19 swing
pase	5 pass	mache	13 walk	leve	20 lift
choute	6 kick	kouri	14 run	naje	21 swim
sève	7 serve	sote kòd	15 hop	plonje	22 dive
mate	8 bounce	kouri sote	16 skip	tire flèch	23 shoot

pouse monte	24 push-up
leve chita	25 sit-up
plonje	26 deep knee bend
vole bra anlè janm louvri	27 jumping jack
fè lakwobat	28 somersault
fè lawou	29 cartwheel
plake	30 handstand

[1–10]
A. _____ the ball!
B. Okay, Coach!

[11–23]
A. Now _____!
B. Like this?
A. Yes.

[24–30]
A. Okay, everybody. I want you to do twenty _____s!
B. Twenty _____s?!
A. That's right.

Do you exercise regularly?
Which exercises do you do?

Be an exercise instructor! Lead your friends in an exercise routine using the actions in this lesson.

ANMIZMAN

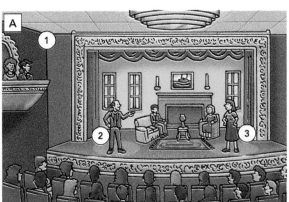

pyès teyat	**A**	**play**
teyat	**1**	theater
aktè	**2**	actor
aktris	**3**	actress
konsè	**B**	**concert**
sal pou konsè	**4**	concert hall
òkès	**5**	orchestra
mizisyen	**6**	musician
mayestwo/chèf òkès	**7**	conductor
djaz	**8**	band

opera	**C**	**opera**
chantè opera	**9**	opera singer
balè	**D**	**ballet**
dansè bale	**10**	ballet dancer
balerin	**11**	ballerina
klib mizik	**E**	**music club**
chantè/chantèz	**12**	singer

sinema	**F**	**movies**
sinema	**13**	(movie) theater
ekran	**14**	(movie) screen
aktris	**15**	actress
aktè	**16**	actor
klib komedi	**G**	**comedy club**
komedyen	**17**	comedian

[A–G]
A. What are you doing this evening?
B. I'm going to { a _____ [A, B, E, G]____ .
                  the _____[C, D, F]____ .

[1–17]
A. What a magnificent _____!
B. I agree.

What kinds of entertainment in this lesson do you like?
What kinds of entertainment are popular in your country?

Who are some of your favorite actors? actresses?
musicians? singers? comedians?

TYPES OF ENTERTAINMENT

DIVÈS ANMIZMAN

A

B

mizik	**A**	**music**
mizik klasik	1	classical music
mizik popilè	2	popular music
mizik konntri	3	country music
mizik wòk	4	rock music
mizik fòlklò	5	folk music

mizik rap	6	rap music
mizik evanjelik	7	gospel music
mizik djaz	8	jazz
mizik blouz	9	blues
mizik blougras	10	bluegrass
ip òp	11	hip hop
mizik rege	12	reggae

dives pyès teyat	**B**	**plays**
dram	13	drama
komedi	14	comedy
trajedi	15	tragedy
komedi mizikal	16	musical (comedy)

sinema	**C**	**movies/films**
dram	**17**	drama
komedi	**18**	comedy
wèstenn	**19**	western
mistè	**20**	mystery
mizikal	**21**	musical
katoun	**22**	cartoon
dokimantè	**23**	documentary
fim avanti	**24**	action movie/ adventure movie
fim lagè	**25**	war movie

fim djab	**26**	horror movie
fim syans	**27**	science fiction movie
fim etranje	**28**	foreign film
pwogram **televizyon**	**D**	**TV programs**
dram	**29**	drama
komedi/ sitcom	**30**	(situation) comedy/ sitcom
pwogram entèvyou/rakont	**31**	talk show

pwogram jwèt	**32**	game show/ quiz show
istwa reyèl	**33**	reality show
feyton	**34**	soap opera
katoun	**35**	cartoon
pwogram timoun	**36**	children's program
pwogram nouvèl	**37**	news program
pwogram espò	**38**	sports program
dokimantè sou lanati	**39**	nature program
pwogram achte	**40**	shopping program

A. What kind of ___[A–D]___ do you like?

B. {
I like ___[1–12]___ .
I like ___[13–40]___ s.

What's your favorite type of music?
Who is your favorite singer? musician?
musical group?

What kind of movies do you like?
Who are your favorite movie stars?
What are the titles of your favorite movies?

What kind of TV programs do you like?
What are your favorite shows?

ENSTRIMAN MIZIK

Enstriman ak kòd		Strings
vyolon	**1**	violin
vyola	**2**	viola
vyolonsèl	**3**	cello
bas	**4**	bass
gita	**5**	(acoustic) guitar
gita elektrik	**6**	electric guitar
bandjo	**7**	banjo
hap	**8**	harp

Enstriman ak van		Woodwinds
pikolo	**9**	piccolo
flit	**10**	flute
klarinèt	**11**	clarinet
obwa	**12**	oboe
flitabèk	**13**	recorder
saksofòn	**14**	saxophone
bason	**15**	bassoon

Enstriman an kwiv		Brass
twonpèt	**16**	trumpet
twonbòn	**17**	trombone
kò konsè	**18**	French horn
kontrebas	**19**	tuba

Pèkisyon		Percussion
tanbou	**20**	drums
senbal	**a**	cymbals
tanbouren	**21**	tambourine
zilofòn	**22**	xylophone

Enstriman ak klavye		Keyboard Instruments
pyano	**23**	piano
pyano elektrik	**24**	electric keyboard
òg	**25**	organ

Lòt enstriman		Other Instruments
akòdeyon	**26**	accordion
amonika	**27**	harmonica

A. Do you play a musical instrument?
B. Yes. I play the **violin**.

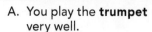

A. You play the **trumpet** very well.
B. Thank you.

A. What's that noise?!
B. That's my son/daughter practicing the **drums**.

Do you play a musical instrument? Which one?

Which instruments are usually in an orchestra? a marching band? a rock group?

Name and describe typical musical instruments in your country.

FÈM AK ZANNIMO LAN FÈM NAN

kay fèm	**1**	farmhouse	kòk	**14**	rooster	mouton	**27**	sheep
fèmye	**2**	farmer	pak kochon	**15**	pig pen	plantasyon fwi	**28**	orchard
jaden legim	**3**	(vegetable) garden	kochon	**16**	pig	pye fwi	**29**	fruit tree
epouvantay	**4**	scarecrow	lakou poul	**17**	chicken coop	plantè/ouvrive	**30**	farm worker
pay	**5**	hay	poul	**18**	chicken	jaden		
ouvriye fèm	**6**	hired hand	poulay	**19**	hen house	alfafa	**31**	alfalfa
anga	**7**	barn	manman poul	**20**	hen	mayi	**32**	corn
ekiri/pak zannimo	**8**	stable	rekòt	**21**	crop	koton	**33**	cotton
chwal	**9**	horse	sistèm awozaj	**22**	irrigation system	diri	**34**	rice
lakou anga	**10**	barnyard	traktè	**23**	tractor	grenn soja	**35**	soybeans
kodenn	**11**	turkey	jaden	**24**	field	ble	**36**	wheat
kabrit	**12**	goat	patiraj	**25**	pasture			
timouton	**13**	lamb	vach	**26**	cow			

[1–30]
A. Where's the _____?
B. In/Next to the _____.

A. The __[9, 11–14, 16, 18, 20, 26]__ s / __[27]__ are loose again!
B. Oh, no! Where are they?
A. They're in the __[1, 3, 7, 8, 10, 15, 17, 19, 24, 25, 28]__.

[31–36]
A. Do you grow _____ on your farm?
B. No. We grow _____.

Tell about farms in your country. What crops and animals are common on these farms?

élan **1** moose	koyòt **9** coyote	tatou **20** armadillo	chen **33** prairie
bwa élan **a** antler	renna **10** fox	chòvsourit **21** bat	andeyò dog
lous blan **2** polar bear	moufèt **11** skunk	vè **22** worm	chat **34** cat
sèf **3** deer	pòkepik **12** porcupine	limas **23** slug	moustach **a** whiske
zago **a** hoof-hooves	pikan **a** quill	makak **24** monkey	ti chat **35** kitten
lou **4** wolf-wolves	lapen **13** rabbit	foumilyè **25** anteater	chen **36** dog
fouri **a** coat/fur	kastò **14** beaver	lama **26** llama	ti chen **37** puppy
lous nwa **5** (black) bear	rat dlo **15** raccoon	jagwa **27** jaguar	amstè **38** hamster
grif **a** claw	oposòm **16** possum/	tach **a** spots	jèbil **39** gerbil
lyon **6** mountain	opossum	sourit **28** mouse-mice	kochondenn **40** guinea pi
lion	chwal **17** horse	rat **29** rat	pwason **41** goldfish
lous bren **7** (grizzly)	ke **a** tail	chipmonk **30** chipmunk	kannari **42** canary
bear	ti chwal **18** pony	ekirèy **31** squirrel	jako **43** parakeet
boufalo **8** buffalo/bison	bourik **19** donkey	gofè **32** gopher	

antilòp	44	antelope
baboun	45	baboon
rinosewòs	46	rhinoceros
kòn		**a** horn
panda	47	panda
oranwoutan	48	orangutan
pantè	49	panther
makak	50	gibbon

tig	51	tiger
pat		**a** paw
chamo	52	camel
bòs		**a** hump
elefan	53	elephant
defans		**a** tusk
twonp		**b** trunk

yèn	54	hyena
lyon	55	lion
krinyè		**a** mane
jiraf	56	giraffe
zèb	57	zebra
ba		**a** stripes
chenpanze	58	chimpanzee

ipopotam	59	hippopotamus
leyopa	60	leopard
goril	61	gorilla
kangouwou	62	kangaroo
pòch		**a** pouch
koala	63	koala (bear)
platipous	64	platypus

[1–33, 44–64]
A. Look at that _____!
B. Wow! That's the biggest _____ I've ever seen!

[34–43]
A. Do you have a pet?
B. Yes. I have a _____.
A. What's your _____'s name?
B. ....

What animals are there where you live?

Is there a zoo near where you live? What animals does it have?

What are some common pets in your country?

If you could be an animal, which animal would you like to be? Why?

Does your culture have any popular folk tales or children's stories about animals? Tell a story you know.

ZWAZO AK ENSÈK

Zwazo		Birds			
wouj gòj	**1**	robin	èg	**10**	eagle
nich	**a**	nest	grif	**a**	claw
ze	**b**	egg	siy	**11**	swan
jeble	**2**	blue jay	wanganègès	**12**	hummingbird
zèl	**a**	wing	kanna	**13**	duck
ke	**b**	tail	bèk	**a**	bill
plim	**c**	feather	grijyou	**14**	sparrow
kadinal	**3**	cardinal	zwa	**15**	goose-geese
graga	**4**	crow	pengwen	**16**	penguin
mwèt	**5**	seagull	flanman	**17**	flamingo
sèpantye	**6**	woodpecker	zwazo gri	**18**	crane
bèk	**a**	beak	sigòy	**19**	stork
pijon	**7**	pigeon	grangozye	**20**	pelican
chwèt	**8**	owl	pan	**21**	peacock
malfini	**9**	hawk	jako	**22**	parrot
			otrich	**23**	ostrich

Ensèk		Insects			
mouch	**24**	fly	arenyen	**33**	spider
kòksinèl	**25**	ladybug	twal arenyen	**a**	web
koukouy	**26**	firefly/	ensèk	**34**	praying
		lightning	lapriyè		mantis
		bug	gèp	**35**	wasp
mit	**27**	moth	myèl	**36**	bee
chenni	**28**	caterpillar	nich myèl	**a**	beehive
kokon	**a**	cocoon	chwal bwa	**37**	grasshopper
papiyon	**29**	butterfly	vonvon	**38**	beetle
tik	**30**	tick	eskòpyon	**39**	scorpion
moustik	**31**	mosquito	milpat	**40**	centipede
demwazèl	**32**	dragonfly	krikèt	**41**	cricket

[1–41]
A. Is that a/an _____?
B. No. I think it's a/an _____.

[24–41]
A. Hold still! There's a _____ on your shirt!
B. Oh! Can you get it off me?
A. There! It's gone!

What birds and insects are there where you live?

Does your culture have any popular folk tales or children's stories about birds or insects? Tell a story you know.

PWASON, BÈT LANMÈ AK REPTIL

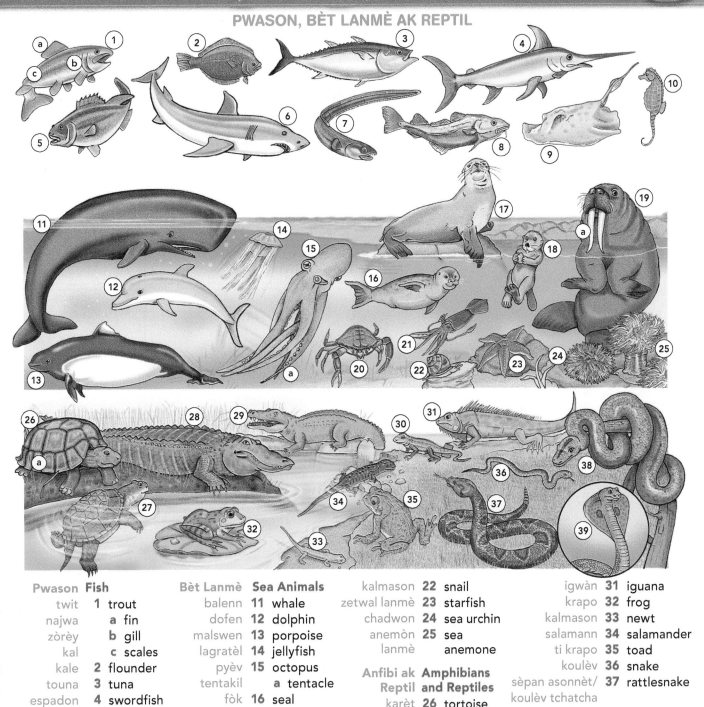

Pwason		Fish
twit	**1**	trout
najwa	**a**	fin
zòrèy	**b**	gill
kal	**c**	scales
kale	**2**	flounder
touna	**3**	tuna
espadon	**4**	swordfish
bas	**5**	bass
reken	**6**	shark
angi	**7**	eel
mori	**8**	cod
rè	**9**	ray/stingray
chwal lanmè	**10**	sea horse

Bèt Lanmè		Sea Animals
balenn	**11**	whale
dofen	**12**	dolphin
malswen	**13**	porpoise
lagratèl	**14**	jellyfish
pyèv	**15**	octopus
tentakil		**a** tentacle
fòk	**16**	seal
otari (fòk)	**17**	sea lion
lout	**18**	otter
mòs	**19**	walrus
defans		**a** tusk
krab	**20**	crab
chatwouj	**21**	squid

kalmason	**22**	snail
zetwal lanmè	**23**	starfish
chadwon	**24**	sea urchin
anemòn lanmè	**25**	sea anemone

Anfibi ak Reptil		Amphibians and Reptiles
karèt	**26**	tortoise
karapas		**a** shell
tòti	**27**	turtle
kayiman	**28**	alligator
kwokodil	**29**	crocodile
leza	**30**	lizard

igwàn	**31**	iguana
krapo	**32**	frog
kalmason	**33**	newt
salamann	**34**	salamander
ti krapo	**35**	toad
koulèv	**36**	snake
sèpan asonnèt/ koulèv tchatcha	**37**	rattlesnake
bowa/gwo koulèv anvlopè	**38**	boa constrictor
sèpanalinèt	**39**	cobra

[1–39]

A. Is that a/an _____?
B. No. I think it's a/an _____.

[26–39]

A. Are there any _____s around here?
B. No. But there are lots of _____!

What fish, sea animals, and reptiles can be found in your country? Which ones are endangered and need to be protected? Why?

In your opinion, which ones are the most interesting? the most beautiful? the most dangerous?

TREES, PLANTS, AND FLOWERS
PYEBWA, PLANT AK FLÈ

pyebwa	**1** tree	dogwoud/	**11** dogwood	chèn	**19** oak	plant	**28** plant
fèy-fèy yo	**2** leaf-leaves	kònye		pye pen	**20** pine	kaktis	**29** cactus-cacti
ti branch	**3** twig	hou	**12** holly	sekoya	**21** redwood	plant	**30** vine
branch	**4** branch	magnolia/	**13** magnolia	sòl	**22** (weeping)	grenpan	
gwo branch	**5** limb	franjipàn		plerè	willow	pwa	**31** poison
twon	**6** trunk	elm/òm	**14** elm	touf bwa	**23** bush	grate	ivy
ekòs	**7** bark	pye seriz	**15** cherry	hou	**24** holly	pwazon	**32** poison suma
rasin	**8** root	pye palmis	**16** palm	frèz	**25** berries	soumak	
zegwi	**9** needle	boulo	**17** birch	ti pyebwa	**26** shrub	bwatchèn	**33** poison oak
pòm pyepen	**10** pine cone	erab	**18** maple	foujè	**27** fern	pwazon	

flè	34	flower	sousi	43	marigold	flè solèy	52	sunflower
petal	35	petal	kannasyon	44	carnation	woukou	53	crocus
tij	36	stem	gadennya	45	gardenia	tilip	54	tulip
bouton flè	37	bud	lis	46	lily	flè jeranyòm	55	geranium
pikan	38	thorn	iris	47	iris	vyolèt	56	violet
zonyon	39	bulb	panse	48	pansy	pwennsetya	57	poinsettia
krizantèm	40	chrysanthemum	petinya	49	petunia	jasmen	58	jasmine
dafodil	41	daffodil	òkide	50	orchid	choublak	59	hibiscus
magerit	42	daisy	wòz	51	rose			

[11–22]
A. What kind of tree is that?
B. I think it's a/an _____ tree.

[31–33]
A. Watch out for the _____ over there!
B. Oh. Thanks for the warning.

[40–57]
A. Look at all the _____s!*
B. They're beautiful!

*With 58 and 59, use: Look at all the ___!

Describe your favorite tree and your favorite flower.

What kinds of trees and flowers grow where you live?

In your country, what flowers do you see at weddings? at funerals? during holidays? in hospital rooms? Tell which flowers people use for different occasions.

ENNÈJI, KONSÈVASYON AK ANVIWÒNMAN

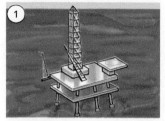

Sous Ennèji		Sources of Energy	Konsèvasyon		Conservation	Pwoblèm Anviwònman		Environmental Problems
luil/lwil	1	oil/petroleum	resiklaj	9	recycle	polisyon lè	13	air pollution
gaz natirèl	2	(natural) gas	konsève ennèji	10	save energy/ conserve energy	polisyon dlo	14	water pollution
chabon	3	coal				dechè toksik	15	hazardous waste/ toxic waste
ennèji atomik	4	nuclear energy						
ennèji solèy	5	solar energy	konsève dlo	11	save water/ conserve water	lapli asid	16	acid rain
fòs idwoelektrik	6	hydroelectric power				radyasyon	17	radiation
van	7	wind				tè a vin pi cho	18	global warming
chalè anndan tè pou fè kouran elektrik	8	geothermal energy	kondui ansanm	12	carpool			

[1–8]

A. In my opinion, _____ will be our best source of energy in the future.

B. I disagree. I think our best source of energy will be _____.

[9–12]

A. Do you _____?

B. Yes. I'm very concerned about the environment.

[13–18]

A. Do you worry about the environment?

B. Yes. I'm very concerned about _____.

What kind of energy do you use to heat your home? to cook? In your opinion, which will be the best source of energy in the future?

Do you practice conservation? What do you do to help the environment?

In your opinion, what is the most serious environmental problem in the world today? Why?

DEZAS NATIRÈL

tranbleman tè	**1** earthquake	
siklòn	**2** hurricane	
anpil lapli	**3** typhoon	
tanpèt nèj	**4** blizzard	
toubiyon	**5** tornado	

inondasyon	**6** flood
sounami	**7** tsunami
sechrès	**8** drought
dife nan fore	**9** forest fire
ensandi/dife sovaj	**10** wildfire

eboulman	**11** landslide
deboulman labou	**12** mudslide
avalanch	**13** avalanche
volkan ki eklate	**14** volcanic eruption

A. Did you hear about the _____ in ....(country)......?
B. Yes, I did. I saw it on the news.

Have you or someone you know ever experienced a natural disaster? Tell about it.

Which natural disasters sometimes happen where you live? How do people prepare for them?

FÒM IDANTIFIKASYON

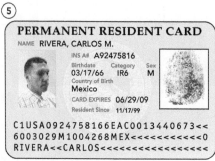

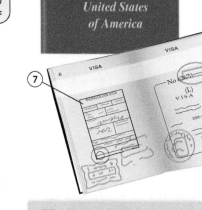

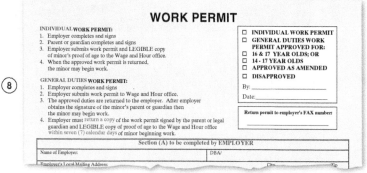

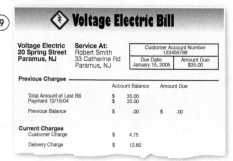

lisans **1** driver's license	kat **5** permanent	pèmi travay **8** work permit
kat sosyal **2** social security card	rezidans resident card	prèv **9** proof of
kat etidyan **3** student I.D. card	pas pò **6** passport	rezidans residence
baj anplwaye **4** employee I.D. badge	viza **7** visa	batistè **10** birth certificate

A. May I see your _____?
B. Yes. Here you are.

A. Oh, no! I can't find my _____!
B. I'll help you look for it.
A. Thanks.

Which forms of identification do you have? When do you need to show them?

GOUVÈNMAN ETAZINI/AMERIKEN

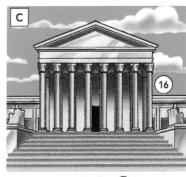

branch	**A**	**legislative branch**
lejislatif		
fè lwa yo	**1**	makes the laws
depite ak senatè	**2**	representatives/ congressmen and congresswomen
kay depite yo	**3**	house of representatives
senatè	**4**	senators
sena	**5**	senate
Kay depite ak senatè	**6**	Capitol Building

pouvwa egzekitiv	**B**	**executive branch**
ranfòse lwa yo	**7**	enforces the laws
prezidan	**8**	president
vis prezidan	**9**	vice-president
kabinè	**10**	cabinet
palè nasyonnal	**11**	White House

pouvwa jidisyè	**C**	**judicial branch**
eksplike lwa yo	**12**	explains the laws
jij an Kasasyon	**13**	Supreme Court justices
prezidan kasasyon	**14**	chief justice
Kasasyon	**15**	Supreme Court
Kay Kasasyon	**16**	Supreme Court Building

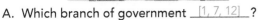

A. Which branch of government __[1, 7, 12]__ ?
B. The __[A, B, C]__ .

A. Who works in the __[A, B, C]__ of the government?
B. The __[2, 4, 8–10, 13, 14]__ .

A. Where do/does the __[2, 4, 8–10, 13, 14]__ work?
B. In the __[6, 11, 16]__ .

A. In which branch of the government is the __[3, 5, 10, 15]__ ?
B. In the __[A, B, C]__ .

Compare the governments of different countries you are familiar with. What are the branches of government?
Who works there? What do they do?

KONSTITISYON AN AK PWOJÈ LWA

A ①

B ③

C ④  ⑤  ⑥  ⑦

D ⑧ 13th 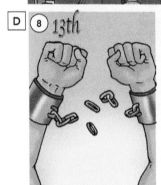 ⑨ 15th  ⑩ 16th  ⑪ 19th  ⑫ 26th

Konstitisyon	**A The Constitution**
premye lwa peyi a	**1** "the supreme law of the land"
Preanbil	**2** the Preamble
Pwojè Lwa	**B The Bill of Rights**
premye 10	**3** the first 10 amendments
ògmantasyon nan	to the Constitution
Konstitisyon an	
Premye Ogmantasyon an	**C The 1st Amendment**
libète pawòl	**4** freedom of speech
libète ekri	**5** freedom of the press
libète relijyon	**6** freedom of religion
libète reyinyon	**7** freedom of assembly

Lòt Ogmantasyon	**D Other Amendments**
fini esklavay	**8** ended slavery
bay nèg Ameriken dwa pou yo vote	**9** gave African-Americans the right to vote
etabli enpo sou lajan ou fè	**10** established income taxes
bay fanm dwa pou yo vote	**11** gave women the right to vote
bay sitwayen ki gen 18 tan ou plis dwa pou yo vote	**12** gave citizens eighteen years and older the right to vote

A. What is ___[A ,B]___?
B. ___[1 ,3]___.

A. Which amendment guarantees people ___[4–7]___?
B. The 1st Amendment.

A. Which amendment ___[8–12]___?
B. The _____ Amendment.

A. What did the _____ Amendment do?
B. It ___[8–12]___.

Describe how people in your community exercise their 1st Amendment rights. What are some examples of freedom of speech? the press? religion? assembly?

Do you have an idea for a new amendment? Tell about it and why you think it's important.

EVÈNMAN NAN ISTWA ETAZINI

TIMELINE

1607	Colonists come to Jamestown, Virginia. Kolon yo rive Jamestown, Virginia.
1620	Pilgrims come to the Plymouth Colony. Pèleren yo vini nan Plymouth Koloni yo.
1775	The Revolutionary War begins. Gè Revolisyon an kòmanse.
1776	The colonies declare their independence. Koloni yo deklare endepandans yo.
1783	The Revolutionary War ends. Gè Revolisyon an fini.
1787	Representatives write the United States Constitution. Manm nan chanm depite yo ekri Konstitisyon Etazini an.
1789	George Washington becomes the first president. George Washington vin premye prezidan.
1791	The Bill of Rights is added to the Constitution. Yo ajoute Pwojè Lwa nan Konstitisyon an.
1861	The Civil War begins. Gè sivil la kòmanse.
1863	President Lincoln signs the Emancipation Proclamation. Prezidan Lincoln siyen Pwoklamasyon Emansipansyon lan.
1865	The Civil War ends. Gè sivil la fini.
1876	Alexander Graham Bell invents the telephone. Alexander Graham Bell envante telefòn.
1879	Thomas Edison invents the lightbulb. Thomas Edison envante anpoul.
1914	World War I (One) begins. Premye Gè Mondyal kòmanse.
1918	World War I (One) ends. Premye Gè Mondyal fini.
1920	Women get the right to vote. Fanm gen dwa vote.
1929	The stock market crashes, and the Great Depression begins. Fayit bous/Stak makèt epi Gwo Depresyon kòmanse.
1939	World War II (Two) begins. Dezyèm Gè Mondyal kòmanse.
1945	World War II (Two) ends. Dezyèm Gè Mondyal fini.
1950	The Korean War begins. Gè Koreyen an kòmanse.
1953	The Korean War ends. Gè Koreyen an fini.
1954	The civil rights movement begins. Mouvman dwa sivil la kòmanse.
1963	The March on Washington takes place. Mach rive Washington lan te fèt.
1964	The Vietnam War begins. Gè Vietnam lan kòmanse.
1969	Astronaut Neil Armstrong lands on the moon. Astwonòt Neil Armstrong rive nan lalin.
1973	The Vietnam War ends. Gè Vietnam lan fini.
1991	The Persian Gulf War occurs. Gè Gòlf Pèsik la rive.
2001	The United States is attacked by terrorists. Teworis atake Etazini.

A. What happened in ....(year)....?
B. ......(Event)....ed.

A. When did .....(event)....?
B. In .....(year)......

In your opinion, which event in this lesson is the most important? Why?

Tell about important events in the history of your country.

JOU FÈT/KONJE

Joudlan	**1**	New Year's Day
Jou Martin Luther King, Jr.	**2**	Martin Luther King, Jr.* Day
Jou dè Valanten	**3**	Valentine's Day
Jou Memoryal	**4**	Memorial Day
Jou Endepandas/ Kat Jiye	**5**	Independence Day/ the Fourth of July
Alowin	**6**	Halloween
Jou Veteran	**7**	Veterans Day
Tanksgivin	**8**	Thanksgiving
Nwèl	**9**	Christmas
Ramadan	**10**	Ramadan
Kwannza	**11**	Kwanzaa
Anouka	**12**	Hanukkah

* Jr. = Junior

A. When is ___[1, 3, 5, 6, 7, 9]___?
B. It's on ......(date)...... .

A. When is ___[2, 4, 8]___?
B. It's in ......(month)...... .

A. When does ___[10–12]___ begin this year?
B. It begins on ......(date)...... .

Which of these holidays do you celebrate? How?

What holidays do people celebrate in your country?

arete	**A**	be arrested	menòt	**3**	handcuffs	avoka	**15** defense
fèmen nan	**B**	be booked at the	Dwa Miranda	**4**	Miranda rights	akize	attorney
biwo polis la		police station	anprent	**5**	fingerprints	prèv	**16** evidence
pran yon	**C**	hire a lawyer/	foto polis	**6**	mug shot/	yisye	**17** bailiff
avoka		hire an attorney			police photo	jiri	**18** jury
parèt nan tribinal	**D**	appear in court	avoka	**7**	lawyer/attorney	kondanasyon	**19** verdict
kapab jije	**E**	stand* trial	jij	**8**	judge	inosan/	**20** innocent/
lage	**F**	be acquitted	defandan	**9**	defendant	pa koupab	not guilty
kondane	**G**	be convicted	lajan	**10**	bail	koupab	**21** guilty
pran santans	**H**	be sentenced	sal tribinal	**11**	courtroom	kondanasyon	**22** sentence
al nan prizon	**I**	go to jail/prison	komisè	**12**	prosecuting	amand	**23** fine
lage	**J**	be released			attorney	jandam	**24** prison guard
sispèk	**1**	suspect	temwen	**13**	witness	prizonye	**25** convict/prisoner/
ofisye polis	**2**	police officer	repòtè tribinal	**14**	court reporter		inmate

*stand-stood

[A–J]

A. Did you hear about ......(name)......?
B. No, I didn't.
A. He/She _____ed.
B. Really? I didn't know that.

[A–J]

A. What happened in the last episode?
B. ......(name of character)...... _____ed.

[1, 2, 7–9, 12–15, 17, 24, 25]

A. Are you the _____?
B. No. I'm the _____.

Tell about the legal system in your country.
Describe what happens after a person is arrested.

Do you watch any crime shows on TV? Which ones?
Tell about an episode you remember.

SITWAYENNTE

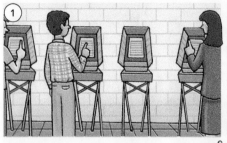

Dwa ak Responsablite Sitwayen	Citizens' Rights and Responsibilities
vote	**1** vote
obeyi lwa	**2** obey laws
peye enpo	**3** pay taxes
patisipe nan yon jiri	**4** serve on a jury
fè pati nan yon kominote	**5** be part of community life
swiv nouvèl pou konn sa k ap pase	**6** follow the news to know about current events
rejistre nan lame	**7** register with the Selective Service System*

* All males in the United States ages 18 to 26 must register with the Selective Service System.

Wout pou yon moun swiv pou vin sitwayen	The Path to Citizenship
ranpli yon aplikasyon pou vin sitwayen	**8** apply for citizenship
aprann zafè gouvènman ak istwa Etazini	**9** learn about U.S. government and history
pran egzamen pou vin sitwayen	**10** take a citizenship test
gen yon entèviou pou natirilizasyon	**11** have a naturalization interview
ale nan yon seremoni natirilizasyon	**12** attend a naturalization ceremony
resite sèman drapo a	**13** recite the Oath of Allegiance

A. Can you name one responsibility of United States citizens?
B. Yes. Citizens should ___[1–7]___.

A. How is your citizenship application coming along?
B. Very well. I ___[8–11]___ed, and now I'm preparing to ___[9–13]___.
A. Good luck!

In your opinion, what are the most important rights and responsibilities of all people in their communities?

In your opinion, should non-citizens have all the same rights as citizens? Why or why not?

ETAZINI AK KANADA

RUSSIA

ARCTIC OCEAN

Chukchi Sea

Norwegian Sea

ICELAND

Bering Sea

Beaufort Sea

GREENLAND

Baffin Bay

Alaska (US)

Yukon Territory

Northwest Territories

Nunavut

PACIFIC OCEAN

British Columbia

Alberta

CANADA

Hudson Bay

Newfoundland and Labrador

Saskatchewan

Manitoba

Québec

Prince Edward Island

New Brunswick

Nova Scotia

Washington

Ontario

Montana

North Dakota

Minnesota

Maine

Ottawa ★

Oregon

Idaho

Wyoming

South Dakota

Wisconsin Michigan

New York

Vermont
New Hampshire
Massachusetts
Rhode Island
Connecticut
New Jersey
Delaware
Maryland
Washington, DC

Nebraska

Iowa

Pennsylvania

Nevada

Utah

Colorado

Kansas

Illinois

Indiana Ohio

West Virginia

California

Arizona

New Mexico

UNITED STATES of AMERICA

Missouri

Oklahoma

Arkansas

Kentucky

Tennessee

Virginia

North Carolina

South Carolina

ATLANTIC OCEAN

Hawaii (US)

Texas

Mississippi

Alabama

Georgia

BERMUDA

Louisiana

Florida

Gulf of Mexico

MEXICO

THE BAHAMAS

CUBA

PUERTO RICO

JAMAICA

HAITI

DOMINICAN REPUBLIC

N
W   E
S

1000 Miles

1000 KM

MEKSIK, AMERIK SANTRAL AK KARAYIB

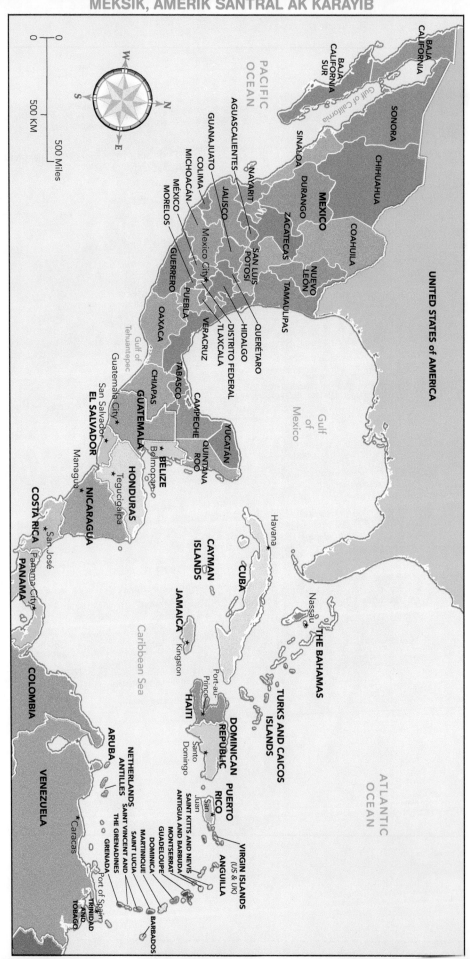

AMERIK SID

Caribbean Sea

Barranquilla
Cartagena•   •Maracaibo   •Valencia   ★Caracas
              Barquisimeto •Caracas

ATLANTIC
OCEAN

VENEZUELA

•Medellín

Georgetown
GUYANA   Paramaribo
            •Cayenne

★Bogotá

SURINAME FRENCH
          GUIANA

•Cali

COLOMBIA

Equator   Equator

Quito
★
ECUADOR   •Belém

•Guayaquil

Gulf of
Guayaquil

Manaus•   Fortaleza•

                                 Teresina•

PERU   BRAZIL

                                               Recife•

★Lima

                                               Salvador•

★La Paz   ★Brasília

BOLIVIA   Goiânia•

Sucre•

                              Belo Horizonte•

                                       Rio de Janeiro•
CHILE   Campinas•
            PARAGUAY   São Paulo•

PACIFIC   Asuncion★   Curitiba•
OCEAN

                   Pôrto Alegre•

ARGENTINA

•Córdoba

Rosario•

Santiago★   URUGUAY

          Buenos Aires★
                   Montevideo

Gulf of San Matías

ATLANTIC
OCEAN

Gulf of
San Jorge

N

W   E

S

0   500 Miles

0   500 KM

FALKLAND
ISLANDS

Strait of Magellan   Port Stanley

SOUTH GEORGIA
ISLAND

LEMONN

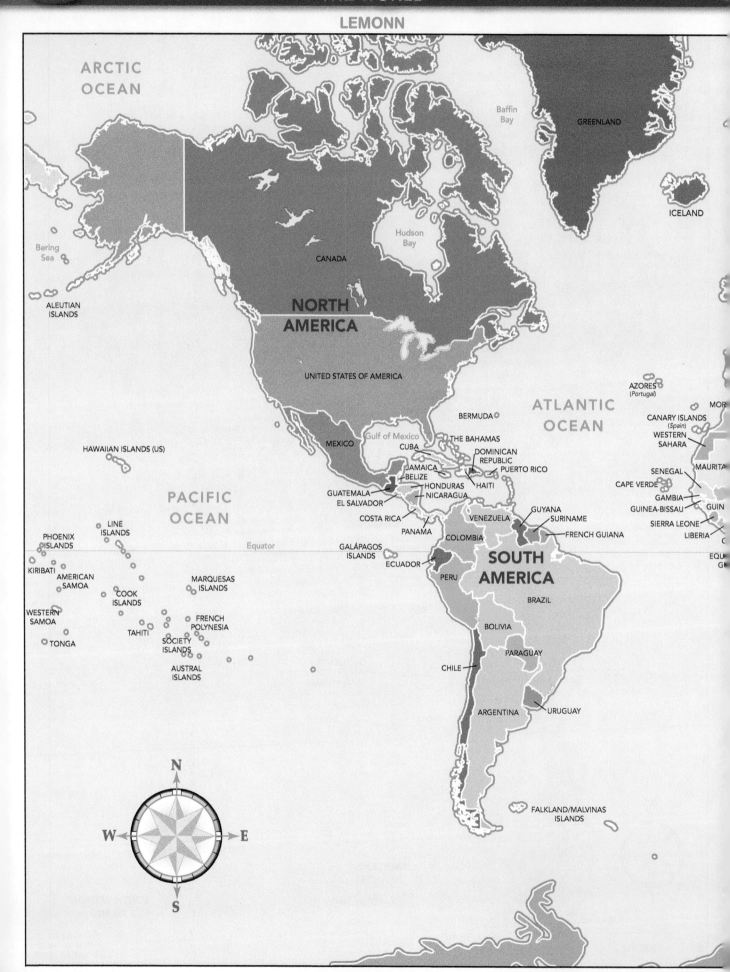

ARCTIC
OCEAN

Baffin
Bay

GREENLAND

ICELAND

Bering
Sea

Hudson
Bay

CANADA

ALEUTIAN
ISLANDS

NORTH
AMERICA

UNITED STATES OF AMERICA

ATLANTIC
OCEAN

AZORES
(Portugal)

MOR

BERMUDA

CANARY ISLANDS
(Spain)
WESTERN
SAHARA

HAWAIIAN ISLANDS (US)

Gulf of Mexico

THE BAHAMAS

MEXICO

CUBA

DOMINICAN
REPUBLIC

PACIFIC

OCEAN

JAMAICA
BELIZE
HONDURAS
NICARAGUA

PUERTO RICO

HAITI

MAURITA

SENEGAL

CAPE VERDE

GAMBIA
GUINEA-BISSAU

GUIN

GUATEMALA
EL SALVADOR

COSTA RICA

PANAMA

GUYANA
SURINAME
FRENCH GUIANA

SIERRA LEONE

LIBERIA

LINE
ISLANDS

PHOENIX
ISLANDS

Equator

GALÁPAGOS
ISLANDS

VENEZUELA

COLOMBIA

ECUADOR

SOUTH
AMERICA

EQU
G

KIRIBATI

AMERICAN
SAMOA

COOK
ISLANDS

MARQUESAS
ISLANDS

PERU

BRAZIL

WESTERN
SAMOA

TAHITI

FRENCH
POLYNESIA

BOLIVIA

TONGA

SOCIETY
ISLANDS

PARAGUAY

CHILE

AUSTRAL
ISLANDS

ARGENTINA

URUGUAY

N

W   E

S

FALKLAND/MALVINAS
ISLANDS

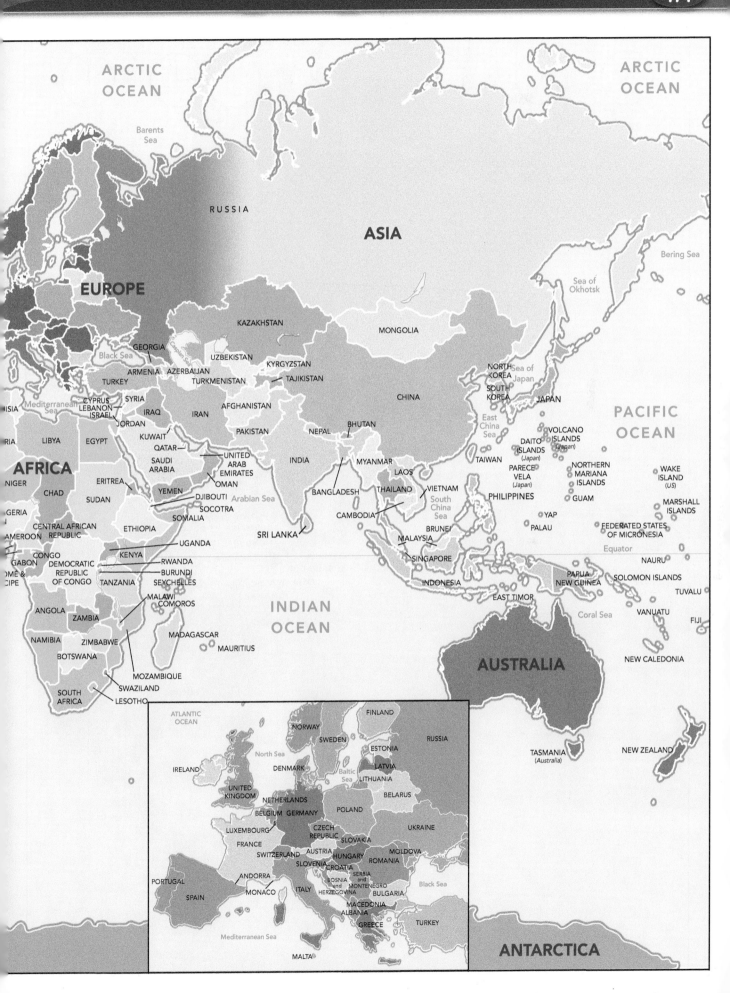

ARCTIC OCEAN

ARCTIC OCEAN

Barents Sea

RUSSIA

ASIA

Bering Sea

EUROPE

Black Sea

Sea of Okhotsk

KAZAKHSTAN

MONGOLIA

GEORGIA

Caspian Sea

UZBEKISTAN

KYRGYZSTAN

NORTH KOREA

Sea of Japan

ARMENIA

AZERBAIJAN

TURKMENISTAN

TAJIKISTAN

SOUTH KOREA

JAPAN

PACIFIC OCEAN

TURKEY

CYPRUS

SYRIA

CHINA

East China Sea

DAITO ISLANDS (Japan)

VOLCANO ISLANDS (Japan)

LEBANON

ISRAEL

IRAQ

IRAN

AFGHANISTAN

TAIWAN

PARECE VELA (Japan)

NORTHERN MARIANA ISLANDS

WAKE ISLAND (US)

JORDAN

KUWAIT

NEPAL

BHUTAN

Mediterranean Sea

LIBYA

EGYPT

QATAR

SAUDI ARABIA

UNITED ARAB EMIRATES

PAKISTAN

INDIA

MYANMAR

LAOS

GUAM

MARSHALL ISLANDS

AFRICA

ERITREA

OMAN

YEMEN

DJIBOUTI

BANGLADESH

THAILAND

VIETNAM

PHILIPPINES

YAP

PALAU

FEDERATED STATES OF MICRONESIA

NIGER

CHAD

SUDAN

SOCOTRA

CAMBODIA

South China Sea

BRUNEI

NIGERIA

CENTRAL AFRICAN REPUBLIC

SOMALIA

ETHIOPIA

Arabian Sea

SRI LANKA

MALAYSIA

SINGAPORE

Equator

NAURU

CAMEROON

CONGO

UGANDA

KENYA

NEW GUINEA

SOLOMON ISLANDS

GABON

DEMOCRATIC REPUBLIC OF CONGO

RWANDA

BURUNDI

TANZANIA

SEYCHELLES

INDONESIA

EAST TIMOR

PAPUA NEW GUINEA

TUVALU

SAO TOME & PRINCIPE

MALAWI

COMOROS

INDIAN OCEAN

Coral Sea

VANUATU

FIJI

ANGOLA

ZAMBIA

MADAGASCAR

MAURITIUS

NEW CALEDONIA

NAMIBIA

ZIMBABWE

BOTSWANA

MOZAMBIQUE

AUSTRALIA

SWAZILAND

SOUTH AFRICA

LESOTHO

TASMANIA (Australia)

NEW ZEALAND

ATLANTIC OCEAN

FINLAND

NORWAY

SWEDEN

RUSSIA

North Sea

ESTONIA

IRELAND

DENMARK

Baltic Sea

LATVIA

LITHUANIA

BELARUS

UNITED KINGDOM

NETHERLANDS

BELGIUM

GERMANY

POLAND

UKRAINE

LUXEMBOURG

CZECH REPUBLIC

SLOVAKIA

FRANCE

AUSTRIA

HUNGARY

MOLDOVA

SWITZERLAND

SLOVENIA

CROATIA

ROMANIA

PORTUGAL

ANDORRA

MONACO

ITALY

SERBIA and MONTENEGRO

BOSNIA and HERZEGOVINA

Black Sea

SPAIN

BULGARIA

MACEDONIA

ALBANIA

GREECE

TURKEY

Mediterranean Sea

MALTA

ANTARCTICA

ZÒN POU LÈ

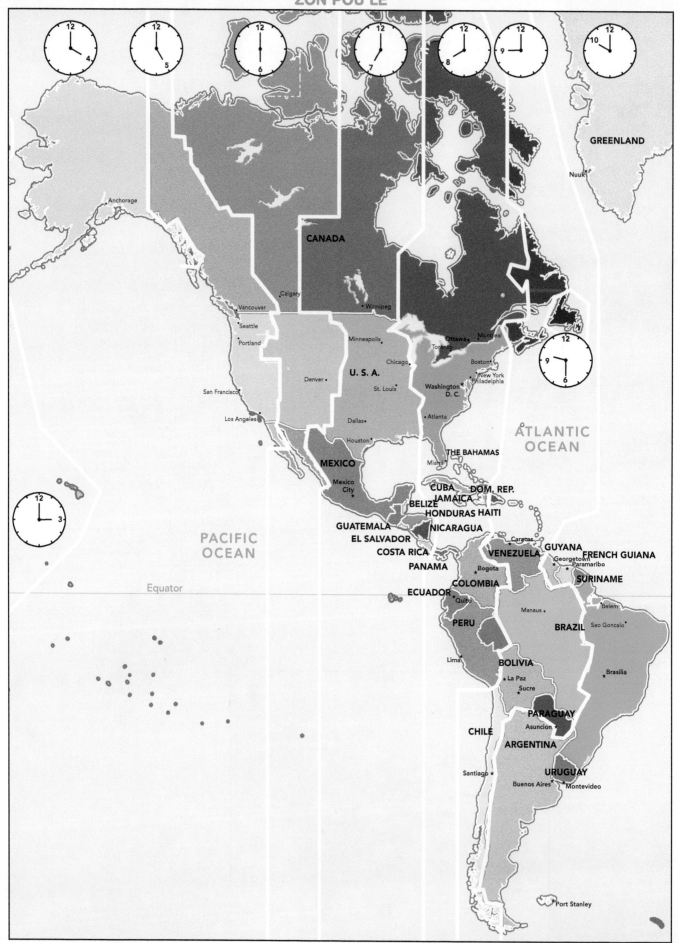

PEYI, NASYONALITE AK LANG

Country	Nationality	Language
Afghanistan	Afghan	Afghan
Argentina	Argentine	Spanish
Australia	Australian	English
Bolivia	Bolivian	Spanish
Brazil	Brazilian	Portuguese
Bulgaria	Bulgarian	Bulgarian
Cambodia	Cambodian	Cambodian
Canada	Canadian	English/French
Chile	Chilean	Spanish
China	Chinese	Chinese
Colombia	Colombian	Spanish
Costa Rica	Costa Rican	Spanish
Cuba	Cuban	Spanish
(The) Czech Republic	Czech	Czech
Denmark	Danish	Danish
(The) Dominican Republic	Dominican	Spanish
Ecuador	Ecuadorian	Spanish
Egypt	Egyptian	Arabic
El Salvador	Salvadorean	Spanish
England	English	English
Estonia	Estonian	Estonian
Ethiopia	Ethiopian	Amharic
Finland	Finnish	Finnish
France	French	French
Germany	German	German
Greece	Greek	Greek
Guatemala	Guatemalan	Spanish
Haiti	Haitian	Haitian Kreyol
Honduras	Honduran	Spanish
Hungary	Hungarian	Hungarian
India	Indian	Hindi
Indonesia	Indonesian	Indonesian
Israel	Israeli	Hebrew

Country	Nationality	Language
Italy	Italian	Italian
Japan	Japanese	Japanese
Jordan	Jordanian	Arabic
Korea	Korean	Korean
Laos	Laotian	Laotian
Latvia	Latvian	Latvian
Lebanon	Lebanese	Arabic
Lithuania	Lithuanian	Lithuanian
Malaysia	Malaysian	Malay
Mexico	Mexican	Spanish
New Zealand	New Zealander	English
Nicaragua	Nicaraguan	Spanish
Norway	Norwegian	Norwegian
Pakistan	Pakistani	Urdu
Panama	Panamanian	Spanish
Peru	Peruvian	Spanish
(The) Philippines	Filipino	Tagalog
Poland	Polish	Polish
Portugal	Portuguese	Portuguese
Puerto Rico	Puerto Rican	Spanish
Romania	Romanian	Romanian
Russia	Russian	Russian
Saudi Arabia	Saudi	Arabic
Slovakia	Slovak	Slovak
Spain	Spanish	Spanish
Sweden	Swedish	Swedish
Switzerland	Swiss	German/French/Italian
Taiwan	Taiwanese	Chinese
Thailand	Thai	Thai
Turkey	Turkish	Turkish
Ukraine	Ukrainian	Ukrainian
(The) United States	American	English
Venezuela	Venezuelan	Spanish
Vietnam	Vietnamese	Vietnamese

A. Where are you from?
B. I'm from **Mexico**.

A. What's your nationality?
B. I'm **Mexican**.

A. What language do you speak?
B. I speak **Spanish**.

Tell about yourself: Where are you from? What's your nationality? What languages do you speak?

Now interview and tell about a friend.

LIS VÈB

Vèb Regilye

Vèb regilye yo gen kat (4) modèl òtograf diferan pou fòm pase ak fòm patisip pase.

1 Ajoute **–ed** nan fen vèb la. Pa egzanp:

> act → acte**d**

act	cook	grill	pass	simmer
add	correct	guard	peel	sort
answer	cough	hand (in)	plant	spell
appear	cover	help	play	sprain
ask	crash	insert	polish	steam
assist	cross (out)	invent	pour	stow
attack	deliver	iron	print	stretch
attend	deposit	kick	reach	surf
bank	design	land	record	swallow
board	discuss	leak	register	talk
boil	dress	learn	relax	turn
box	drill	lengthen	repair	twist
brainstorm	dust	lift	repeat	unload
broil	edit	listen	request	vacuum
brush	end	load	respond	vomit
burn	enter	look	rest	walk
burp	establish	lower	return	wash
carpool	explain	mark	roast	watch
cash	faint	match	rock	wax
check	fasten	mix	saute	weed
clean	fix	mow	scratch	whiten
clear	floss	obey	seat	work
collect	fold	open	select	
comb	follow	paint	shorten	
construct	form	park	sign	

2 Ajoute **–d** nan yon vèb ki fini an **–e**. Pa egzanp:

> assemble → assemble**d**

assemble	declare	grate	pronounce	shave
bake	describe	hire	prune	slice
balance	dislocate	manage	raise	sneeze
barbecue	dive	measure	rake	state
bathe	dribble	microwave	recite	style
bounce	enforce	move	recycle	supervise
browse	erase	nurse	remove	translate
bruise	examine	operate	revise	type
bubble	exchange	organize	rinse	underline
change	exercise	overdose	save	unscramble
circle	experience	practice	scrape	use
close	file	prepare	serve	vote
combine	gargle	produce	share	wheeze

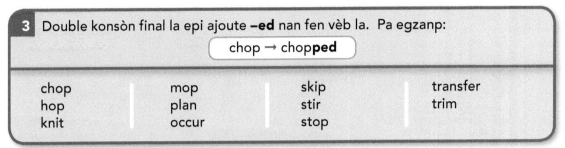

3 Double konsòn final la epi ajoute **–ed** nan fen vèb la. Pa egzanp:

chop → chop**ped**

chop	mop	skip	transfer
hop	plan	stir	trim
knit	occur	stop	

4 Retire –y final la epi ajoute **–ied** nan fen vèb la. Pa egzanp:

apply → appl**ied**

apply	dry	fry	study
copy	empty	stir-fry	try

Vèb Iregilye

Vèb sa yo gen fòm tan pase iregilye ak/oswa fòm patisip pase.

be	was/were	been		know	knew	known
beat	beat	beaten		leave	left	left
become	became	become		let	let	let
bend	bent	bent		make	made	made
begin	began	begun		meet	met	met
bleed	bled	bled		pay	paid	paid
break	broke	broken		put	put	put
bring	brought	brought		read	read	read
build	built	built		rewrite	rewrote	rewritten
buy	bought	bought		run	ran	run
catch	caught	caught		ring	rang	rung
choose	chose	chosen		say	said	said
come	came	come		see	saw	seen
cut	cut	cut		sell	sold	sold
do	did	done		set	set	set
draw	drew	drawn		shoot	shot	shot
drink	drank	drunk		sing	sang	sung
drive	drove	driven		sit	sat	sat
eat	ate	eaten		sleep	slept	slept
fall	fell	fallen		speak	spoke	spoken
feed	fed	fed		stand	stood	stood
fly	flew	flown		sweep	swept	swept
get	got	gotten		swim	swam	swum
give	gave	given		swing	swung	swung
go	went	gone		take	took	taken
grow	grew	grown		teach	taught	taught
hang	hung	hung		throw	threw	thrown
have	had	had		understand	understood	understood
hit	hit	hit		withdraw	withdrew	withdrawn
hold	held	held		write	wrote	written
hurt	hurt	hurt				

VOKABILÈ KREYÒL AYISYEN

Nimewo an karaktè gra a endike paj kote mo a parèt. Nimewo ki vin annapre a endike pozisyon mo a nan pòtre a ak nan lis mo ki nan paj la. Pa egzanp, "address 1-5" endike pozisyon mo a se sou paj 1 epi mo a gen nimewo 5.

VOKABILÈ ANGLE

The bold number indicates the page(s) on which the word appears. The number that follows indicates the word's location in the illustration and in the word list on the page. For example, "address **1**-5" indicates that the word address is on page 1 and is item number 5.

3-point turn **130**-25
35 millimeter camera **77**-14
A.M. **16**
A.V. crew **104**-12
abdomen **86**-25
above **8**-1
accelerator **127**-73
accordion **150**-26
account **80**-E
account number **81**-2b
accountant **112**-1
Ace™ bandage **90**-12
acid rain **158**-16
acorn squash **49**-13
acoustic guitar **150**-5
acquitted **165**-F
across **129**-7
acrylic paint **135**-31
act **116**-1
action figure **79**-12
action movie **149**-24
activities director **84**-12
actor **112**-2, **147**-2,15
actress **112**-3, **147**-3,16
acupuncturist **96**-15
acute angle **106**-20a
ad **118**-A
adapter **77**-13
add **58**-10, **163**
adding machine **77**-11, **119**-13
addition **105**
address **1**-5
adhesive bandage **90**-3
adhesive tape **90**-9
adjective **107**-5
administrative assistant **119**-22
adult **42**-7
adult school **101**-5
adventure movie **149**-24
adverb **107**-7
aerogramme **82**-3
afraid **47**-27
African-American **162**-9
afternoon **19**-5
aftershave **99**-25
aftershave lotion **99**-25
age **42**
AIDS **91**-25
air **126**-48
air bag **127**-49
air conditioner **28**-28, **127**-67
air conditioning **31**-21
air filter **126**-32
air freshener **26**-25
air letter **82**-3
air pollution **158**-13
air pump **126**-41
air purifier **94**-11
air sickness bag **132**-18
air tank **145**-18
airplane **132**-23
aisle **55**-1, **132**-7

aisle seat **132**-10
alarm clock **23**-17
alcohol **93**-10
alfalfa **151**-31
algebra **105**
allergic reaction **91**-7
allergist **96**-5
alligator **155**-28
alternator **126**-38
aluminum foil **54**-12
ambulance **84**-8
amendment **162**-3
American cheese **52**-10
ammonia **32**-14
amphibians **155**
amusement park **136**-5
anesthesiologist **97**-17
anesthetic **93**-F
angry **47**-17
ankle **87**-48
ankle socks **71**-10
anniversary **18**-27
annoyed **46**-16
answer **6**-20, **7**-51,52,54
answer sheet **7**-54
answer the question **6**-19, **7**-48
answering machine **77**-6
antacid tablets **95**-8
anteater **152**-25
antelope **153**-44
antenna **126**-14
antibiotic ointment **90**-7
antihistamine cream **90**-11
antipasto **64**-10
antipasto plate **64**-10
antiseptic cleansing wipe **90**-4
antler **152**-1a
ants **30**-11c
apartment ads **28**-1
apartment building **20**-1
apartment listings **28**-2
apartment number **1**-8
apex **106**-19a
apostrophe **107**-12
appear in court **165**-D
appetizers **64**
apple **48**-1
apple juice **51**-15
apple pie **64**-25
appliance repairperson **30**-E
application form **118**-F
apply for a loan **80**-F
apply for citizenship **166**-8
appointment **18**-28
appointment book **120**-6
apricot **48**-7
April **18**-16
aquarium **136**-14
archery **141**-S
architect **112**-4
area code **1**-12

arithmetic **105**
arm **86**-28
armadillo **152**-20
armchair **21**-29
armrest **127**-82
around **129**-4
arrested **165**-A
arrival and departure board **124**-13
arrival and departure monitor **131**-5
art **103**-19
art gallery **136**-2
arteries **87**-68
artichoke **49**-27
article **107**-4
artist **112**-5
ask a question **6**-17
ask about the benefits **118**-K
ask about the salary **118**-J
ask *you* some questions about *your* health **92**-E
asparagus **49**-7
aspirin **90**-13, **95**-1
assault **85**-11
assemble **116**-2
assembler **112**-6
assembly **162**-7
assembly line **121**-4
assist **116**-3
assistant principal **102**-6
asteroid **111**-11
asthma **91**-18
astronaut **111**-30
astronomer **111**-27
astronomy **111**, **135**-S
athletic shoes **69**-17
athletic supporter **68**-10
atlas **83**-28
ATM **80**-12
ATM card **80**-6
ATM machine **80**-12
attack **163**
attend a naturalization ceremony **166**-12
attorney **165**-7
audio cassette **76**-25
audiologist **96**-9
audiotape **76**-25, **83**-16
auditorium **102**-K
August **18**-20
aunt **3**-2
author **83**-3
autobiography **108**-7
automatic transmission **127**-74
autumn **19**-29
available **118**-6
avalanche **159**-13
average height **42**-15
average weight **42**-18
avocado **48**-14
ax **34**-3

baboon **153**-45
baby **2**-7, **10**-5, **42**-2
baby backpack **25**-31
baby carriage **25**-21
baby carrier **25**-23
baby cereal **54**-15
baby food **54**-16, **100**-1
baby frontpack **25**-30
baby lotion **100**-16
baby monitor **25**-2
baby powder **100**-11
baby products **54**
baby seat **25**-26
baby shampoo **100**-14
baby wipes **100**-10
babysitter **112**-7
back **86**-27
back door **27**-21
back support **123**-7
backache **88**-5
backboard **143**-22
backgammon **135**-37
backhoe **122**-18
backpack **70**-25, **139**-10
backup light **126**-20
backyard **27**
bacon **50**-14, **61**-12
bacon, lettuce, and tomato sandwich **61**-27
bad **44**-32
badminton **140**-J
badminton racket **140**-20
bag **56**-1, **132**-C
bagel **61**-3
baggage **131**-17
baggage carousel **131**-16
baggage cart **131**-18
baggage claim **131**-D, 15
baggage claim area **131**-15
baggage claim check **131**-21
baggage compartment **124**-10
bagger **55**-14
baggy **72**-4
bail **165**-10
bailiff **165**-17
bait **145**-29
bake **58**-15, **116**-4
baked chicken **64**-14
baked goods **53**
baked potato **64**-18
baker **112**-8
bakery **36**-1
baking products **53**
balance **110**-17
balance beam **141**-39
balance the checkbook **81**-16
balcony **28**-21
bald **43**-35
ballerina **147**-11
ballet **147**-D
ballet dancer **147**-10
ballfield **137**-11, **142**-2,4

TI KOZE SOU KREYÒL AYISYEN

Kreyòl Ayisyen se yon lang endepandan ki ekri jan yo pale li men dapre regleman gramè pa li. Li chita sou vokabilè franse sèzyèm rive dizwityèm syèk epi li sèvi ak regleman gramè lang nan peyi Lwès Afrik yo. Li se yon lang nasyonnal tout ayisyen ak pi fò etranje kap viv ann Ayiti pale. Li menm ak franse se de lang ofisyèl peyi a. Ayisyen yo ki fèt oswa kap viv nan peyi etranje pran plezi pale li anpil. Gen ayisyen ki rele lang yo *ayisyen*.

- Òtograf Kreyòl Ayisyen chita sou kat prensip fondalnatal:
  1. Yon siy pou chak son
  2. Menm siy nan pou menm son an
  3. Nanpwen lèt ki bèbè
  4. Chak lèt rete nan wòl li

- Gen dis manman son. Se vwayèl lang nan. Men ki jan yo ekri siy yo:

  a (*papa*), **an** (*manman*),
  e (*bebe*), **è** (*bèbè*), **en** (*benyen*), **i** (*diri*),
  o (*bobo*), **ò** (*bòzò*), **on** (*bonbon*), **ou** (*moumou*).

Sonje: **an en on ou** se vwayèl ak yon sèl son. Avèk aksan grav (`) sou **a e o** ou gen **àn èn òn** kòm nan **kà**nva (*kanvas*), **pòs**lèn (*china*), **mò**n (*hill*).

Son vwayèl yo pa janm chanje.

- **Alfabèt Kreyòl Ayisyen**

a	an	b	ch	d	e	è	en	f	g
h	i	j	k	l	m	n	o	ò	on
ou	p	r	s	t	ui	v	w	y	z

Sonje: Nan alfabèt kreyòl ayisyen pa gen **u** men **ui**, pa gen **c** men **ch**, pa gen konsòn **q** ak **x**. Lèt **g** toujou gen son di tankou nan go. Pa pwononse lèt **j** kòm si li te gen lèt **d** devan li. Pa woule lèt **r** devan vwayèl. Li pa parèt nan fen okenn silab. Se **w** ki ranplase **r** devan **o ò on ou**: wo (*high*), wòb (*dress*), won (*round*), wou (*hoe*). Lèt **s** toujou pwononse **ès**, li pa janmen sèvi pou **z**.

- Gen senk pwonon: **mwen ou li nou yo** Yo toujou apre non ak vèb sòf lè yo se sijè.

- Gen senk atik defini sengilye: **la lan nan a an** Yo sèvi selon jan mo ki devan yo fini. Sèl atik defini pliryèl se **yo**.

Menm mo a ka non ak vèb oswa non ak akjektif.

Word by Word respekte òtograf ofisyèl kreyòl ayisyen an ki tabli depi 31 janvye 1980.

Woje E. Saven

Haitian Kreyol is an autonomous and phonetic spelling language based on 16th to 18th century lexical French and syntax principles of West African languages. It is the national language spoken by the entire population of Haiti and by most foreigners living in that country. One of the two official languages of Haiti, with French, it is also the congenial language used by people of Haitian descent born or living abroad. It is written the way it is pronounced, but it has its own grammatical rules. Some Haitians called their language *ayisyen*.

- Haitian Kreyol orthography has four fundamental principles:
  1. One sign for each sound
  2. The same sign for the same sound
  3. No silent letters
  4. Each letter has its own function

- It has ten basic sounds and they are the vowels:

  a (*father*), **an** (*manman*),
  e (*say*), **è** (*get*), **en** (*lens*), **i** (*sea*),
  o (*low*), **ò** (*ought*), **on** (*don't*), **ou** (*two*).

Note: **an en on ou** always function as single vowels with one sound each. The grave accent (`) modifies the sound of **a e o** which become:

  à as in kànva, **è** as in pòslèn, **ò** as in mòn.

The vowel sounds never change.

- **Haitian Kreyol Alphabet**

a	an	b	ch	d	e	è	en	f	g
h	i	j	k	l	m	n	o	ò	on
ou	p	r	s	t	ui	v	w	y	z

Note: In the Haitian Kreyol alphabet there is no **u** but **ui**, no **c** but **ch**, and no consonants **q** and **x**. The letter **g** is always pronounced like the **g** in *go*. The letter **j** is pronounced like the **j** in *Jan*. Do not roll the letter **r**. It does not occur at the end of any syllable. It is replaced by **w** before **o ò on ou**: wo (*high*), wòb (*dress*), won (*round*), wou (*hoe*). Letter **s** is always **ess**, it never substitutes for **z**.

- The five pronouns: **mwen ou li nou yo** always come after nouns and verbs except when they are subjects.

- The five singular definite articles: **la lan nan a an**, are used according to the ending of the word which precedes them. The only plural definite is **yo**.

The same word is often noun, verb or adjective.

Word by Word conforms to the Haitian Kreyol spelling, established since January 31, 1980.

Roger E. Savain